Low Carb Diet Cookbook

Copyright-All Rights Reserved

This book has copyright protection.You can use the book for personal purpose.You should not see,use,alter,distribute,quote,take excerpts or paraphrase in part or whole the material contained in this book without obtaining the permission of the author first.

Introduction

Introducing the "Low Carb Diet Cookbook": Embrace a delicious and wholesome culinary journey with this collection of mouthwatering recipes carefully curated to support your low-carb lifestyle. Whether you're new to the world of low-carb eating or a seasoned enthusiast, this cookbook is designed to tantalize your taste buds while promoting a healthier and more balanced approach to cooking.

Within these pages, you'll find a diverse array of dishes that cater to a wide range of tastes and preferences. From hearty breakfasts to savory lunches, and from delectable dinners to indulgent desserts, each recipe has been thoughtfully crafted to minimize carbohydrates without compromising on flavor.

Discover the art of creating sumptuous meals using fresh, nutrient-packed ingredients that will keep you energized and satisfied throughout your day. Learn how to transform classic favorites into low-carb wonders and explore innovative new dishes that will surprise and delight your family and friends.

Whether you're seeking to shed a few pounds, manage blood sugar levels, or simply adopt a healthier lifestyle, the "Low Carb Diet Cookbook" empowers you to embrace culinary creativity without feeling restricted. So, grab your apron and let's embark on a culinary adventure that celebrates both wellness and taste in equal measure. Get ready to savor every bite and nourish your body with these delightful low-carb creations. Let the cooking journey begin!

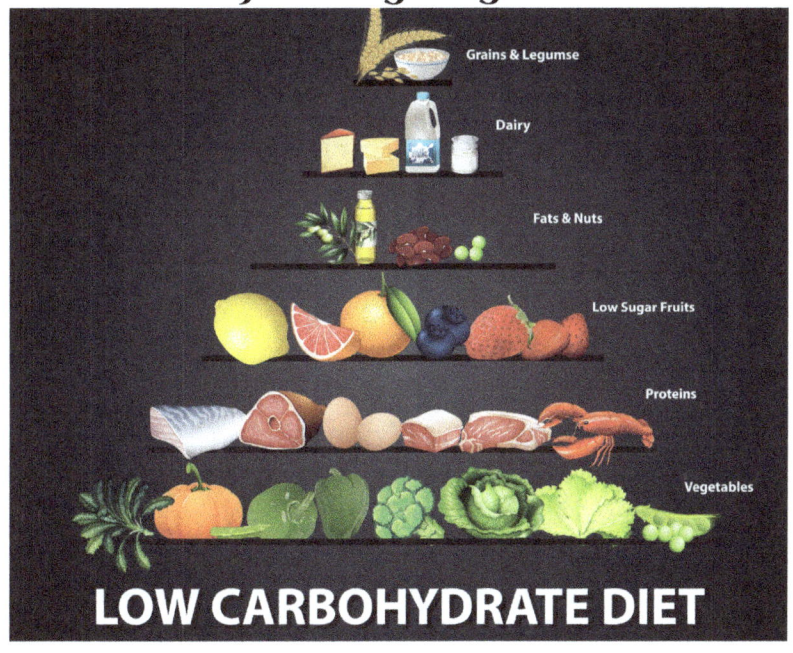

Contents

Introduction ....

Chapter One ....
Delicious Breakfasts

Chapter Two ....
Scrumptious Salads

Chapter Tree ....
Soups & Stews

Chapter Four ....
Snacks & Sides

Chapter Five ....
Desserts

Chapter Six ....
Seafood

Avocado and Black Bean Eggs

Ingredients:

2 ripe avocados
4 large eggs
1/2 cup black beans, drained and rinsed
1 tablespoon olive oil
1/2 teaspoon ground cumin
1/2 teaspoon paprika
Salt and pepper to taste
Fresh cilantro (coriander) for garnish (optional)
Salsa or hot sauce (optional, for serving)

Instructions:

Preheat your oven to 375°F (190°C).
Cut the avocados in half and remove the pits. Scoop out a little extra flesh from each half to create a larger well for the egg.
In a baking dish or oven-safe pan, drizzle the olive oil. Place the avocado halves in the dish, so they don't tip over.
Sprinkle some ground cumin, paprika, salt, and pepper over each avocado half.
Now, carefully crack an egg into each avocado half, being cautious not to spill the egg white. The egg should fit into the well you created by scooping out some avocado flesh.
Spoon some black beans over each avocado half, distributing them evenly around the egg.
Bake in the preheated oven for about 15-20 minutes or until the egg whites are set, but the yolks are still slightly runny. If you prefer fully cooked yolks, bake for a few extra minutes.
Once done, remove the avocado and black bean eggs from the oven.
Garnish with fresh cilantro (coriander) if desired, and serve with a side of salsa or hot sauce for an extra kick.
This dish makes for a satisfying and nutritious low-carb breakfast or brunch option. Enjoy!

Banana oat pancakes

Ingredients:

2 ripe bananas
2 large eggs
1/2 cup almond flour
1/2 cup rolled oats (use gluten-free oats if needed)
1 teaspoon baking powder
1/2 teaspoon ground cinnamon (optional)
Pinch of salt
1/4 cup unsweetened almond milk (or any milk of your choice)
1 teaspoon vanilla extract
Coconut oil or butter for greasing the pan
Fresh berries or sliced bananas for topping (optional)

Instructions:

In a blender or food processor, add the ripe bananas, eggs, almond flour, rolled oats, baking powder, ground cinnamon (if using), and a pinch of salt.
Blend the mixture until it becomes smooth and well combined. If the batter appears too thick, you can add a little almond milk to reach the desired consistency.
Let the batter sit for a few minutes to allow the oats to soften slightly.
While the batter rests, heat a non-stick skillet or griddle over medium heat. Add a small amount of coconut oil or butter to grease the pan.
Once the pan is hot, pour about 1/4 cup of the pancake batter onto the skillet for each pancake. You can make them smaller or larger, depending on your preference.
Cook the pancakes for 2-3 minutes on each side, or until they are golden brown and cooked through.
Transfer the cooked pancakes to a plate and repeat the process with the remaining batter.
Serve the low-carb banana oat pancakes with fresh berries or sliced bananas on top, if desired. You can also drizzle some sugar-free maple syrup or a dollop of Greek yogurt for extra flavor.
These pancakes are not only low in carbs but also packed with fiber and nutrients from the bananas and oats. They make for a delightful and guilt-free breakfast or snack option!
Enjoy!

Healthy pepper, tomato & ham omelette

Ingredients:

4 large eggs
1/4 cup diced bell peppers (any color you prefer)
1/4 cup diced tomatoes
1/4 cup diced cooked ham (you can also use turkey or chicken ham)
2 tablespoons chopped green onions (scallions)
1/4 cup shredded cheddar cheese (or any cheese of your choice)
1 tablespoon olive oil or butter
Salt and pepper to taste
Fresh parsley or cilantro for garnish (optional)

Instructions:

In a bowl, whisk the eggs until they are well beaten. Season with a pinch of salt and pepper.
Heat the olive oil or butter in a non-stick skillet over medium heat.
Add the diced bell peppers and sauté for 2-3 minutes until they start to soften.
Stir in the diced tomatoes and cook for an additional 1-2 minutes until they release some of their juices.
Add the diced ham to the skillet and stir it with the vegetables for another minute to heat it through.
Pour the beaten eggs evenly over the vegetables and ham in the skillet. Tilt the pan to spread the eggs evenly.
Cook the omelette for a few minutes, occasionally lifting the edges gently with a spatula to allow the uncooked eggs to flow underneath.
Sprinkle the chopped green onions and shredded cheddar cheese over half of the omelette.
Once the eggs are mostly set but still slightly runny on top, carefully fold the omelette in half, covering the filling.
Cook for an additional minute or until the cheese has melted, and the omelette is cooked through.
Slide the omelette onto a serving plate, and garnish with fresh parsley or cilantro if desired.
This healthy pepper, tomato, and ham omelette is not only low in carbs but also packed with protein and vegetables, making it a perfect low-carb breakfast or brunch option. Enjoy it on its own or with a side of fresh salad for a satisfying and nutritious meal!

Chocolate chia pudding

Ingredients:

1/4 cup chia seeds
1 cup unsweetened almond milk (or any milk of your choice)
2 tablespoons unsweetened cocoa powder
1-2 tablespoons low-carb sweetener (such as stevia, erythritol, or monk fruit) - adjust to your taste
1/2 teaspoon vanilla extract
Pinch of salt
Optional toppings: sliced strawberries, raspberries, shredded coconut, chopped nuts, or sugar-free chocolate chips.

Instructions:

In a medium-sized bowl, whisk together the unsweetened almond milk, cocoa powder, low-carb sweetener, vanilla extract, and a pinch of salt. Mix until the cocoa powder is fully dissolved and everything is well combined.
Add the chia seeds to the mixture and stir thoroughly to make sure they are evenly distributed.
Let the mixture rest for about 5 minutes, then stir it again to prevent clumping. This step helps ensure a smooth consistency in your pudding.
Cover the bowl with plastic wrap or a lid and refrigerate the chocolate chia mixture for at least 3-4 hours or preferably overnight. During this time, the chia seeds will absorb the liquid and create a thick, pudding-like texture.
Before serving, give the chia pudding a good stir to break up any lumps that may have formed. If the pudding is too thick, you can add a little more almond milk to reach your desired consistency.
Divide the chocolate chia pudding into serving bowls or glasses.
Optional: Top the pudding with sliced strawberries, raspberries, shredded coconut, chopped nuts, or sugar-free chocolate chips for added flavor and texture.
This low-carb chocolate chia pudding is a fantastic dessert or snack option. It's rich, creamy, and satisfying while being packed with nutrients from chia seeds and having minimal impact on blood sugar levels due to its low-carb nature. Enjoy it guilt-free!

Tofu scramble

Ingredients:

1 block of firm tofu (about 14 oz)
2 tablespoons olive oil or coconut oil
1/2 small onion, finely chopped
1/2 bell pepper (any color), diced
1-2 cloves garlic, minced
2 tablespoons nutritional yeast (optional, for a cheesy flavor)
1 teaspoon ground turmeric (for color and flavor)
1/2 teaspoon ground cumin
1/2 teaspoon paprika
Salt and pepper to taste
Fresh parsley or cilantro for garnish (optional)

Instructions:

Drain the tofu and pat it dry with paper towels. Crumble the tofu into small pieces with your hands, similar to the texture of scrambled eggs.
In a large skillet or frying pan, heat the olive oil over medium heat.
Add the chopped onion and diced bell pepper to the pan and sauté for 2-3 minutes until they start to soften.
Stir in the minced garlic and cook for another 30 seconds until fragrant.
Add the crumbled tofu to the skillet, spreading it out evenly.
Sprinkle the nutritional yeast, ground turmeric, ground cumin, and paprika over the tofu. These spices will add color and flavor, giving the tofu a taste similar to scrambled eggs.
Season the tofu scramble with salt and pepper to your liking. Remember that the nutritional yeast also adds some saltiness, so adjust accordingly.
Stir the tofu mixture gently but thoroughly to coat the tofu with the spices and distribute the vegetables evenly.
Cook the tofu scramble for about 5-7 minutes, stirring occasionally. This allows the flavors to meld and the tofu to develop a slightly crispy texture.
Once the tofu is heated through and has a texture similar to scrambled eggs, remove the skillet from the heat.
Garnish the tofu scramble with fresh parsley or cilantro if desired.
Serve your low-carb tofu scramble with a side of avocado, some sautéed greens, or low-carb tortillas for a satisfying and nutritious breakfast or brunch option. It's a fantastic plant-based alternative to traditional scrambled eggs and a great way to incorporate more protein into your diet!

Mushroom brunch

Ingredients:

4 large portobello mushrooms (or any mushroom of your choice)
4 large eggs
1/2 cup baby spinach or kale
1/4 cup diced bell peppers (any color)
2 tablespoons diced red onion
2 cloves garlic, minced
2 tablespoons olive oil
Salt and pepper to taste
Fresh herbs for garnish (e.g., parsley, chives, or basil)

Instructions:

Preheat your oven to 375°F (190°C).
Carefully remove the stems from the portobello mushrooms and gently scrape out the gills using a spoon. This creates a hollow space for the filling.
In a skillet over medium heat, add 1 tablespoon of olive oil. Sauté the diced red onion and minced garlic until they become fragrant and slightly softened.
Add the diced bell peppers to the skillet and continue sautéing for another 2-3 minutes until they start to soften.
Stir in the baby spinach or kale and cook until wilted. Season with salt and pepper to taste.
In a separate non-stick skillet, add the remaining 1 tablespoon of olive oil over medium heat. Place the portobello mushrooms, hollow side up, on the skillet.
Divide the sautéed vegetable mixture evenly among the mushrooms, filling up the hollow space.
Carefully crack an egg into the center of each mushroom, on top of the vegetable filling.
Transfer the skillet with the stuffed mushrooms to the preheated oven and bake for about 12-15 minutes, or until the egg whites are set, but the yolks are still slightly runny.
Once the eggs are cooked to your desired level, remove the skillet from the oven.
Garnish the mushroom brunch with fresh herbs, such as parsley, chives, or basil.
Serve the delicious low-carb Mushroom Brunch as a nutritious and filling meal. The combination of savory mushrooms, nutrient-rich vegetables, and perfectly cooked eggs makes it a fantastic option for brunch or any time of the day!

Chocolate porridge

Ingredients:

1/4 cup chia seeds
1 cup unsweetened almond milk (or any milk of your choice)
2 tablespoons unsweetened cocoa powder
1-2 tablespoons low-carb sweetener (such as stevia, erythritol, or monk fruit) - adjust to your taste
1/2 teaspoon vanilla extract
Pinch of salt
Optional toppings: sliced strawberries, raspberries, unsweetened shredded coconut, chopped nuts, or a dollop of whipped cream (all in moderation to keep it low-carb)

Instructions:

In a medium-sized bowl, whisk together the unsweetened almond milk, cocoa powder, low-carb sweetener, vanilla extract, and a pinch of salt. Make sure the cocoa powder is fully dissolved and everything is well combined.
Add the chia seeds to the mixture and stir thoroughly to make sure they are evenly distributed.
Let the mixture rest for about 5 minutes, then stir it again to prevent clumping. This step helps ensure a smooth consistency in your chocolate porridge.
Cover the bowl with plastic wrap or a lid and refrigerate the mixture for at least 3-4 hours or preferably overnight. During this time, the chia seeds will absorb the liquid and create a thick, porridge-like texture.
Before serving, give the chocolate porridge a good stir to break up any lumps that may have formed. If the porridge is too thick, you can add a little more almond milk to reach your desired consistency.
Divide the chocolate porridge into serving bowls.
Optional: Top the porridge with sliced strawberries, raspberries, unsweetened shredded coconut, chopped nuts, or a dollop of whipped cream for added flavor and texture.
This low-carb chocolate porridge is a fantastic breakfast or dessert option. It's rich, creamy, and satisfying while being packed with fiber and nutrients from chia seeds. Enjoy this guilt-free treat any time you crave something chocolatey and comforting!

Healthy cookies

Ingredients:

1 cup almond flour
1/4 cup coconut flour
1/4 cup unsweetened shredded coconut
1/4 cup chopped nuts (e.g., almonds, walnuts, or pecans)
1/4 cup sugar-free chocolate chips or dark chocolate chunks (at least 70% cocoa)
1/4 cup coconut oil, melted
2 large eggs
1/4 cup low-carb sweetener (such as stevia, erythritol, or monk fruit) - adjust to your taste
1 teaspoon vanilla extract
1/2 teaspoon baking powder
Pinch of salt

Instructions:

Preheat your oven to 350°F (175°C) and line a baking sheet with parchment paper.
In a large mixing bowl, combine the almond flour, coconut flour, unsweetened shredded coconut, chopped nuts, sugar-free chocolate chips, baking powder, and a pinch of salt. Mix everything together until well combined.
In a separate bowl, whisk together the melted coconut oil, eggs, low-carb sweetener, and vanilla extract until smooth.
Pour the wet ingredients into the dry ingredients and stir until a thick cookie dough forms. If the dough is too sticky, you can refrigerate it for about 15 minutes to make it easier to handle.
Take small portions of the cookie dough and roll them into balls. Place the balls on the prepared baking sheet and flatten them slightly with the back of a fork.
Bake the cookies in the preheated oven for about 10-12 minutes or until they turn golden brown around the edges.
Once baked, remove the cookies from the oven and let them cool on the baking sheet for a few minutes before transferring them to a wire rack to cool completely.
Store the healthy cookies in an airtight container at room temperature for up to 1 week.
Enjoy these low-carb healthy cookies as a guilt-free treat! They are packed with wholesome ingredients and free from refined sugars, making them a perfect option for anyone looking to satisfy their sweet cravings while keeping carbs in check.

Breakfast burrito

Ingredients:

2 large eggs
1 tablespoon olive oil or butter
1/4 cup diced bell peppers (any color)
1/4 cup diced onions
1/4 cup diced tomatoes
1/4 cup cooked and crumbled breakfast sausage or bacon (optional)
1/4 cup shredded cheddar cheese (or any cheese of your choice)
2 large low-carb tortillas (look for ones with fewer carbs and higher fiber content)
Salt and pepper to taste
Salsa or hot sauce (optional, for serving)

Instructions:

In a bowl, whisk the eggs until well beaten. Season with a pinch of salt and pepper.
Heat the olive oil or butter in a non-stick skillet over medium heat.
Add the diced bell peppers and onions to the skillet and sauté until they start to soften.
Stir in the diced tomatoes and cook for another minute or two until they release some of their juices.
If using breakfast sausage or bacon, add it to the skillet and cook until heated through.
Pour the beaten eggs into the skillet with the vegetables and sausage/bacon, if using. Stir everything together and cook until the eggs are scrambled and fully cooked.
Warm the low-carb tortillas in the microwave or in a separate skillet for a few seconds to make them pliable.
Divide the scrambled egg mixture evenly between the two tortillas, placing it in the center of each tortilla.
Sprinkle the shredded cheddar cheese over the eggs on each tortilla.
Fold in the sides of the tortillas and then roll them up tightly, creating your breakfast burritos.
If desired, you can lightly toast the burritos in a clean skillet for a minute or two to make them extra crispy.
Serve the low-carb breakfast burritos with salsa or hot sauce on the side for added flavor.
These low-carb breakfast burritos are a great way to start your day with a delicious and satisfying meal. You can customize them by adding other low-carb ingredients like avocado, spinach, or mushrooms to suit your taste preferences. Enjoy!

Blueberry & banana power smoothie

Ingredients:

1/2 cup frozen blueberries
1/2 ripe banana
1 cup unsweetened almond milk (or any milk of your choice)
1 tablespoon almond butter (or any nut butter you prefer)
1 tablespoon chia seeds
1/2 teaspoon vanilla extract
A pinch of cinnamon (optional, for added flavor)
Ice cubes (optional, if you prefer a colder and thicker smoothie)
Low-carb sweetener (such as stevia, erythritol, or monk fruit) - adjust to your taste (optional, depending on the sweetness of the fruits)

Instructions:

In a blender, combine the frozen blueberries, ripe banana, almond milk, almond butter, chia seeds, vanilla extract, and cinnamon (if using).
If you prefer a colder and thicker smoothie, you can also add a few ice cubes to the blender.
Blend all the ingredients until you get a smooth and creamy consistency.
Taste the smoothie and add low-carb sweetener if needed to achieve your desired level of sweetness. The ripeness of the banana and the sweetness of the blueberries may already provide enough natural sweetness for some people.
Pour the Blueberry & Banana Power Smoothie into a glass and enjoy it immediately!
This low-carb smoothie is not only delicious but also packed with nutrients from the blueberries, banana, almond butter, and chia seeds. It's a fantastic choice for a quick and nutritious breakfast or a refreshing snack to power up your day!

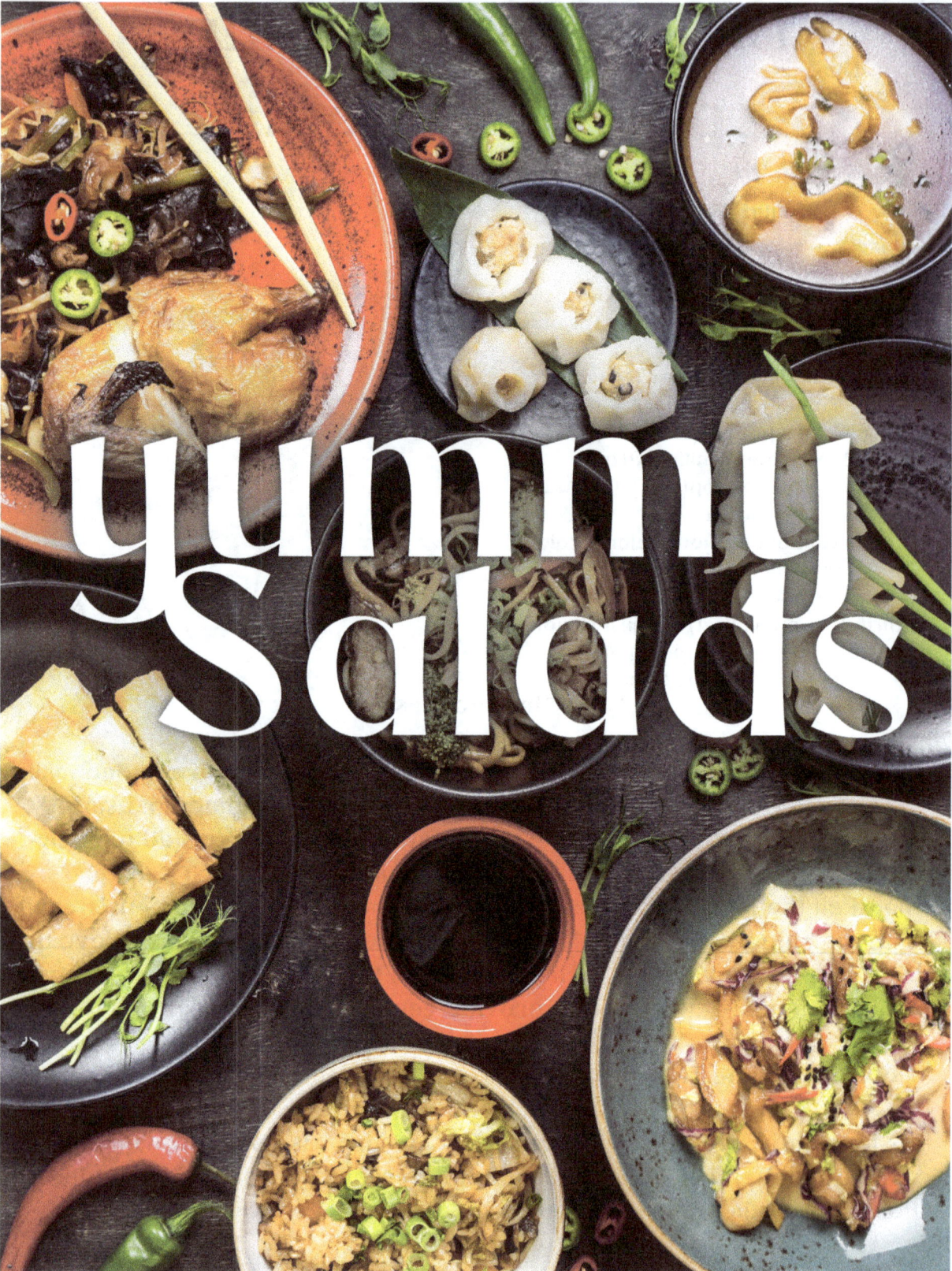

Chopped Power Salad with Chicken

Ingredients for the Salad:

2 cups cooked and shredded chicken breast (grilled, baked, or rotisserie chicken works well)
4 cups mixed salad greens (such as spinach, kale, arugula, and/or romaine)
1 cup cherry tomatoes, halved
1 cucumber, diced
1/2 red bell pepper, diced
1/4 cup thinly sliced red onion
1/4 cup crumbled feta cheese (optional)
2 tablespoons chopped fresh herbs (e.g., parsley, cilantro, or basil)

Ingredients for the Dressing:

3 tablespoons extra-virgin olive oil
1 tablespoon lemon juice
1 clove garlic, minced
1/2 teaspoon Dijon mustard
Salt and pepper to taste

Instructions:

In a large salad bowl, combine the cooked and shredded chicken breast with the mixed salad greens.
Add the halved cherry tomatoes, diced cucumber, diced red bell pepper, and thinly sliced red onion to the bowl.
If using, sprinkle the crumbled feta cheese over the salad.
In a small bowl or jar, whisk together the extra-virgin olive oil, lemon juice, minced garlic, Dijon mustard, salt, and pepper until well combined.
Drizzle the dressing over the chopped power salad and toss everything together until the ingredients are evenly coated with the dressing.
Taste the salad and adjust the seasonings if needed.
Sprinkle the chopped fresh herbs over the salad for an extra burst of flavor.
Serve the Chopped Power Salad with Chicken immediately as a satisfying and nutritious low-carb meal!
This salad is packed with protein from the chicken and a variety of fresh vegetables, making it a well-rounded and healthy option for a low-carb lunch or dinner. Feel free to customize the salad with your favorite low-carb toppings and dressings to suit your taste preferences. Enjoy!

Beet Salad

Ingredients:

2 medium-sized beets, roasted, peeled, and diced (see instructions below for roasting beets)
4 cups mixed salad greens (such as arugula, spinach, or lettuce)
1/4 cup crumbled goat cheese or feta cheese
1/4 cup chopped walnuts or pecans
2 tablespoons balsamic vinegar
2 tablespoons extra-virgin olive oil
1 teaspoon Dijon mustard
Salt and pepper to taste

Instructions for Roasting Beets:

Preheat your oven to 400°F (200°C).
Wash the beets thoroughly and trim off the tops and roots.
Wrap each beet in aluminum foil and place them on a baking sheet.
Roast the beets in the preheated oven for about 45 minutes to 1 hour, or until they are tender when pierced with a fork.
Remove the beets from the oven and let them cool for a few minutes.
Once the beets are cool enough to handle, peel off the skin using your fingers or a peeler. Dice the roasted beets into bite-sized pieces.

Instructions for the Beet Salad:

In a large salad bowl, combine the diced roasted beets with the mixed salad greens.
Add the crumbled goat cheese or feta cheese and chopped walnuts or pecans to the bowl.
In a small bowl, whisk together the balsamic vinegar, extra-virgin olive oil, Dijon mustard, salt, and pepper until well combined.
Drizzle the dressing over the beet salad and toss everything together until the ingredients are evenly coated with the dressing.
Taste the salad and adjust the seasonings if needed.
Serve the Beet Salad immediately as a refreshing and nutritious low-carb side dish or light meal.

This Beet Salad is not only low in carbs but also packed with flavor and nutrients from the roasted beets, mixed greens, cheese, and nuts. It's a beautiful and tasty addition to any meal or a lovely standalone salad for a light and healthy lunch! Enjoy!

Cucumber, Tomato & Feta Salad with Balsamic Dressing

Ingredients:

2 medium cucumbers, diced
2 cups cherry tomatoes, halved
1/2 cup crumbled feta cheese
2 tablespoons chopped fresh parsley or basil
2 tablespoons extra-virgin olive oil
2 tablespoons balsamic vinegar
1 teaspoon Dijon mustard
Salt and pepper to taste

Instructions:

In a large salad bowl, combine the diced cucumbers and halved cherry tomatoes.
Add the crumbled feta cheese and chopped fresh parsley or basil to the bowl.
In a small bowl, whisk together the extra-virgin olive oil, balsamic vinegar, Dijon mustard, salt, and pepper until well combined.
Drizzle the balsamic dressing over the salad and toss everything together until the ingredients are evenly coated with the dressing.
Taste the salad and adjust the seasonings if needed.
Serve the Classic Cucumber, Tomato & Feta Salad immediately as a refreshing and nutritious low-carb side dish or light meal.

Carrot-Cucumber Salad

Ingredients:

2 large carrots, peeled and grated
1 large cucumber, thinly sliced
2 tablespoons chopped fresh cilantro or parsley
2 tablespoons extra-virgin olive oil
1 tablespoon apple cider vinegar or white vinegar
1 teaspoon honey (or low-carb sweetener of your choice)
1/2 teaspoon ground cumin
Salt and pepper to taste
Optional: a pinch of red pepper flakes for some heat

Instructions:

In a large salad bowl, combine the grated carrots and thinly sliced cucumber. Add the chopped fresh cilantro or parsley to the bowl.
In a small bowl, whisk together the extra-virgin olive oil, apple cider vinegar, honey (or low-carb sweetener), ground cumin, salt, and pepper until well combined.
Optional: If you like a little heat, add a pinch of red pepper flakes to the dressing.
Drizzle the dressing over the carrot-cucumber salad and toss everything together until the vegetables are evenly coated with the dressing.
Taste the salad and adjust the seasonings if needed.
Serve the Carrot-Cucumber Salad immediately as a light and refreshing low-carb side dish or as a crunchy and nutritious addition to your meals.
This Carrot-Cucumber Salad is not only low in carbs but also packed with vitamins and minerals from the fresh vegetables. The combination of flavors and textures makes it a delightful and healthy option for any occasion! Enjoy!

Shrimp Cobb Salad with Dijon Dressing

Ingredients for the Salad:

1 pound cooked shrimp, peeled and deveined
6 cups mixed salad greens (such as romaine, spinach, or arugula)
1 cup cherry tomatoes, halved
1 avocado, diced
4 hard-boiled eggs, sliced
4 slices cooked bacon, crumbled
1/4 cup crumbled feta cheese (optional)
2 tablespoons chopped fresh chives or green onions

Ingredients for the Dijon Dressing:

3 tablespoons extra-virgin olive oil
1 tablespoon white wine vinegar or apple cider vinegar
1 tablespoon Dijon mustard
1 clove garlic, minced
Salt and pepper to taste

Instructions:

In a large salad bowl, arrange the mixed salad greens as the base of the Shrimp Cobb Salad.
Arrange the cooked shrimp, halved cherry tomatoes, diced avocado, sliced hard-boiled eggs, and crumbled bacon on top of the salad greens.
If using, sprinkle the crumbled feta cheese over the salad.
In a small bowl or jar, whisk together the extra-virgin olive oil, vinegar, Dijon mustard, minced garlic, salt, and pepper until well combined.
Drizzle the Dijon dressing over the Shrimp Cobb Salad.
Sprinkle the chopped fresh chives or green onions over the salad for an extra burst of flavor.
Toss the salad gently to combine all the ingredients and coat them with the dressing.
Serve the Shrimp Cobb Salad immediately as a satisfying and nutritious low-carb meal!
This salad is loaded with protein from the shrimp and eggs, healthy fats from the avocado, and plenty of fresh vegetables, making it a well-rounded and delicious low-carb option for lunch or dinner. Enjoy this flavorful and filling Shrimp Cobb Salad with Dijon Dressing!

Mixed Vegetable Salad with Lime Dressing

Ingredients for the Salad:

2 cups mixed salad greens (such as spinach, arugula, and lettuce)
1 cup cherry tomatoes, halved
1 cucumber, diced
1 bell pepper (any color), diced
1/2 red onion, thinly sliced
1/4 cup sliced black olives (optional)
1/4 cup crumbled feta cheese (optional)
2 tablespoons chopped fresh parsley or cilantro

Ingredients for the Lime Dressing:

3 tablespoons extra-virgin olive oil
2 tablespoons fresh lime juice
1 teaspoon honey (or low-carb sweetener of your choice)
1 clove garlic, minced
Salt and pepper to taste

Instructions:

In a large salad bowl, combine the mixed salad greens, halved cherry tomatoes, diced cucumber, diced bell pepper, and thinly sliced red onion.
If using, add the sliced black olives and crumbled feta cheese to the salad.
In a small bowl or jar, whisk together the extra-virgin olive oil, fresh lime juice, honey (or low-carb sweetener), minced garlic, salt, and pepper until well combined.
Drizzle the Lime Dressing over the mixed vegetable salad.
Sprinkle the chopped fresh parsley or cilantro over the salad for an extra burst of flavor.
Toss the salad gently to combine all the ingredients and coat them with the lime dressing.
Taste the salad and adjust the seasonings if needed.
Serve the Mixed Vegetable Salad with Lime Dressing immediately as a light and refreshing low-carb side dish or as a healthy and colorful addition to your meals.
This Mixed Vegetable Salad with Lime Dressing is not only low in carbs but also packed with vitamins, minerals, and antioxidants from the fresh vegetables. The zesty lime dressing adds a tangy and delightful flavor to the salad. Enjoy this nutritious and delicious salad!

Creamy Pesto Chicken Salad

Ingredients:

2 cups cooked and shredded chicken (rotisserie chicken works well)
1/4 cup mayonnaise (you can use a low-carb or avocado-based mayo if preferred)
2 tablespoons homemade or store-bought basil pesto
1/4 cup diced red bell pepper
1/4 cup diced celery
2 tablespoons chopped fresh basil
Salt and pepper to taste
Optional: a squeeze of lemon juice for extra freshness

Instructions:

In a large mixing bowl, combine the cooked and shredded chicken with the diced red bell pepper and diced celery.
In a separate small bowl, mix the mayonnaise and basil pesto together until well combined.
Pour the creamy pesto dressing over the chicken and vegetables in the large bowl.
Add the chopped fresh basil to the bowl.
Season the chicken salad with salt and pepper to your taste preference.
Optional: For a touch of brightness, squeeze some lemon juice over the salad.
Toss all the ingredients together until the chicken and vegetables are evenly coated with the creamy pesto dressing.
Taste the salad and adjust the seasonings if needed.
Serve the Creamy Pesto Chicken Salad immediately as a flavorful and satisfying low-carb meal.
This creamy pesto chicken salad is not only low in carbs but also packed with flavor and protein from the chicken and basil pesto. Enjoy it on its own, as a filling for lettuce wraps, or as a delicious topping for low-carb crackers or sliced vegetables. It's a perfect option for a quick and easy lunch or dinner!

Vinaigrette Coleslaw

Ingredients:

4 cups shredded cabbage (green or purple cabbage, or a mix of both)
1 large carrot, grated
2 green onions, thinly sliced
2 tablespoons chopped fresh parsley or cilantro

For the Vinaigrette Dressing:

3 tablespoons extra-virgin olive oil
2 tablespoons apple cider vinegar
1 teaspoon Dijon mustard
1 teaspoon low-carb sweetener (such as stevia, erythritol, or monk fruit) - adjust to your taste
Salt and pepper to taste

Instructions:

In a large salad bowl, combine the shredded cabbage, grated carrot, thinly sliced green onions, and chopped fresh parsley or cilantro.
In a small bowl or jar, whisk together the extra-virgin olive oil, apple cider vinegar, Dijon mustard, low-carb sweetener, salt, and pepper until well combined.
Drizzle the vinaigrette dressing over the coleslaw mixture.
Toss the ingredients together until the cabbage, carrot, and other vegetables are evenly coated with the vinaigrette dressing.
Taste the coleslaw and adjust the seasonings if needed.
Cover the bowl with plastic wrap and refrigerate the coleslaw for at least 30 minutes to allow the flavors to meld and the vegetables to marinate.
Give the coleslaw a good stir before serving.
Serve the Vinaigrette Coleslaw as a refreshing and crunchy low-carb side dish or as a flavorful addition to your meals.
This Vinaigrette Coleslaw is a light and tangy alternative to traditional creamy coleslaw and is perfect for those following a low-carb lifestyle. It's great for picnics, barbecues, or as a side dish for any meal. Enjoy the fresh and zesty flavors of this coleslaw!

Avocado Caprese Salad

Ingredients:

2 ripe avocados, sliced
2 medium ripe tomatoes, sliced
4-6 ounces fresh mozzarella cheese, sliced
Fresh basil leaves
Extra-virgin olive oil
Balsamic glaze or balsamic reduction (optional, for drizzling)
Salt and pepper to taste

Instructions:

Arrange the avocado slices, tomato slices, and fresh mozzarella slices on a serving platter, alternating them to create a visually appealing pattern.
Tuck fresh basil leaves between the slices of avocado, tomato, and mozzarella.
Drizzle extra-virgin olive oil over the salad, making sure to coat all the ingredients lightly.
If desired, drizzle balsamic glaze or balsamic reduction over the Avocado Caprese Salad for a touch of sweetness and tanginess.
Season the salad with a pinch of salt and freshly ground black pepper to taste.
Serve the Avocado Caprese Salad immediately as a refreshing and tasty low-carb appetizer or side dish.
This Avocado Caprese Salad is not only low in carbs but also packed with fresh flavors and nutritious ingredients. It's a fantastic option for a light and healthy snack or as a vibrant and colorful addition to your meals. Enjoy the creamy avocado with the classic combination of tomatoes, mozzarella, and basil in this delightful salad!

Tuna Salad with Egg

Ingredients:

2 cans (5 ounces each) of tuna in water, drained
4 hard-boiled eggs, chopped
1/4 cup diced celery
1/4 cup diced red onion
1/4 cup mayonnaise (you can use a low-carb or avocado-based mayo if preferred)
1 tablespoon Dijon mustard
1 tablespoon freshly squeezed lemon juice
1 tablespoon chopped fresh parsley or dill
Salt and pepper to taste
Optional: Lettuce leaves or low-carb tortilla wraps for serving

Instructions:

In a large mixing bowl, combine the drained tuna, chopped hard-boiled eggs, diced celery, and diced red onion.
In a separate small bowl, mix the mayonnaise, Dijon mustard, and freshly squeezed lemon juice until well combined.
Pour the mayo-mustard dressing over the tuna and egg mixture.
Add the chopped fresh parsley or dill to the bowl.
Season the tuna salad with salt and pepper to your taste preference.
Toss all the ingredients together until the tuna and eggs are evenly coated with the dressing.
Optional: Serve the tuna salad with egg over a bed of lettuce leaves or in low-carb tortilla wraps for a delicious and satisfying low-carb meal.
Enjoy the Tuna Salad with Egg immediately, or refrigerate it for later. It's a perfect option for a quick and easy lunch or dinner!
This tuna salad with egg is not only low in carbs but also packed with protein and healthy fats, making it a nutritious and filling choice for anyone looking to maintain a low-carb lifestyle. Enjoy this flavorful and satisfying salad on its own or as a tasty filling for lettuce wraps or low-carb wraps.

Salmon & Avocado Salad

Ingredients:

2 cups cooked salmon (grilled, baked, or poached), flaked
1 ripe avocado, diced
1 cup mixed salad greens (such as arugula, spinach, or lettuce)
1/4 cup cherry tomatoes, halved
2 tablespoons diced red onion
2 tablespoons chopped fresh dill or cilantro
2 tablespoons extra-virgin olive oil
1 tablespoon freshly squeezed lemon juice
Salt and pepper to taste

Instructions:

In a large salad bowl, combine the flaked cooked salmon, diced avocado, mixed salad greens, halved cherry tomatoes, diced red onion, and chopped fresh dill or cilantro.
In a small bowl, whisk together the extra-virgin olive oil and freshly squeezed lemon juice until well combined.
Drizzle the dressing over the salmon and avocado salad.
Season the salad with salt and pepper to your taste preference.
Toss all the ingredients together gently until the salmon and avocado are evenly coated with the dressing.
Serve the Salmon & Avocado Salad immediately as a flavorful and nutritious low-carb meal.
This Salmon & Avocado Salad is not only low in carbs but also packed with healthy fats, omega-3 fatty acids, and essential nutrients from the salmon and avocado. It's a fantastic option for a light and refreshing lunch or dinner, and the combination of flavors and textures is sure to please your taste buds! Enjoy!

Avocado Tuna Salad

Ingredients:

2 cans (5 ounces each) of tuna in water, drained
1 ripe avocado, diced
1/4 cup diced celery
1/4 cup diced red onion
1/4 cup diced cucumber
2 tablespoons chopped fresh parsley or cilantro
2 tablespoons mayonnaise (you can use a low-carb or avocado-based mayo if preferred)
1 tablespoon Dijon mustard
1 tablespoon freshly squeezed lemon juice
Salt and pepper to taste

Instructions:

In a large mixing bowl, combine the drained tuna, diced avocado, diced celery, diced red onion, diced cucumber, and chopped fresh parsley or cilantro.
In a separate small bowl, mix the mayonnaise, Dijon mustard, and freshly squeezed lemon juice until well combined.
Pour the mayo-mustard dressing over the tuna and avocado mixture.
Season the salad with salt and pepper to your taste preference.
Gently toss all the ingredients together until the tuna and avocado are evenly coated with the dressing.
Optional: Serve the Avocado Tuna Salad on a bed of lettuce leaves, in low-carb tortilla wraps, or on cucumber slices for a low-carb and refreshing meal.
Enjoy the Avocado Tuna Salad immediately, or refrigerate it for later. It's a perfect option for a quick and satisfying low-carb lunch or dinner!
This Avocado Tuna Salad is not only low in carbs but also packed with protein, healthy fats, and essential nutrients from the tuna and avocado. It's a creamy, flavorful, and nourishing salad that will keep you feeling satisfied and energized. Customize it with your favorite low-carb toppings and enjoy!

Spinach Salad with Warm Maple Dressing

Ingredients for the Salad:

4 cups fresh spinach leaves
1/4 cup thinly sliced red onion
1/4 cup crumbled feta cheese (optional)
1/4 cup chopped pecans or walnuts (lightly toasted, if preferred)
1/4 cup dried cranberries or sliced strawberries (optional, for a touch of sweetness and color)

Ingredients for the Warm Maple Dressing:

2 tablespoons olive oil
1 tablespoon apple cider vinegar
1 tablespoon sugar-free maple syrup (or regular maple syrup if not strictly low-carb)
1 teaspoon Dijon mustard
Salt and pepper to taste

Instructions:

In a large salad bowl, combine the fresh spinach leaves, thinly sliced red onion, crumbled feta cheese (if using), chopped pecans or walnuts, and dried cranberries or sliced strawberries (if using).
In a small saucepan, heat the olive oil over low heat.
Whisk in the apple cider vinegar, sugar-free maple syrup (or regular maple syrup), Dijon mustard, salt, and pepper until well combined.
Continue to heat the dressing gently, stirring occasionally, until it becomes warm. Be careful not to boil it.
Pour the warm maple dressing over the spinach salad.
Toss the salad gently to coat all the ingredients with the warm dressing.
Serve the Spinach Salad with Warm Maple Dressing immediately as a delightful and nutritious low-carb side dish or light meal.
This Spinach Salad with Warm Maple Dressing is not only low in carbs but also packed with nutrients, flavors, and textures. The warm maple dressing adds a touch of sweetness and richness to the fresh and vibrant spinach salad. Enjoy this delightful combination of ingredients for a satisfying and healthy meal!

Soup & Stews

Turkey Chili

Ingredients:

1 lb ground turkey
1 tablespoon olive oil
1 small onion, diced
2 cloves garlic, minced
1 red bell pepper, diced
1 green bell pepper, diced
1 can (14 oz) diced tomatoes
1 can (14 oz) tomato sauce
1 can (14 oz) kidney beans, drained and rinsed (optional, omit for lower carb content)
1 cup chicken or vegetable broth
2 tablespoons chili powder
1 teaspoon cumin
1/2 teaspoon paprika
1/2 teaspoon dried oregano
Salt and pepper to taste
Optional toppings: shredded cheese, diced avocado, chopped cilantro, sour cream (use low-fat or Greek yogurt for lower carb options)

Instructions:

In a large pot or Dutch oven, heat the olive oil over medium heat.
Add the diced onion and sauté until softened, about 2-3 minutes.
Add the minced garlic and sauté for another 1 minute, until fragrant.
Add the ground turkey to the pot and cook, breaking it up with a spoon, until it's browned and cooked through.
Add the diced red and green bell peppers to the pot and cook for 2-3 minutes until they start to soften.
Stir in the chili powder, cumin, paprika, dried oregano, salt, and pepper. Mix well to coat the turkey and vegetables with the spices.
Pour in the diced tomatoes, tomato sauce, and chicken or vegetable broth. If using kidney beans, add them to the pot as well.
Bring the chili to a simmer, then reduce the heat to low, cover the pot, and let it simmer for 20-25 minutes, allowing the flavors to meld together.
Taste the chili and adjust the seasonings as needed.
Serve the low-carb Turkey Chili hot, garnished with your favorite toppings, such as shredded cheese, diced avocado, chopped cilantro, or sour cream.
This Turkey Chili is a hearty and satisfying dish that's low in carbs and packed with protein. It's perfect for a comforting and flavorful meal, especially during colder days. Enjoy!

Keto Chicken Tortilla Soup

Ingredients:

1 lb boneless, skinless chicken breasts or thighs, cooked and shredded
2 tablespoons olive oil
1 small onion, diced
2 cloves garlic, minced
1 jalapeño pepper, seeds removed and finely diced (optional, adjust to your spice preference)
1 can (14 oz) diced tomatoes
4 cups chicken broth
1 teaspoon chili powder
1 teaspoon ground cumin
1/2 teaspoon paprika
Salt and pepper to taste
1/4 cup chopped fresh cilantro
Juice of 1 lime
Optional toppings: sliced avocado, shredded cheese, sour cream, chopped green onions, and pork rinds or low-carb tortilla chips for a crunchy texture

Instructions:

In a large pot or Dutch oven, heat the olive oil over medium heat.
Add the diced onion and sauté until softened, about 2-3 minutes.
Add the minced garlic and diced jalapeño pepper (if using), and sauté for another 1-2 minutes until fragrant.
Pour in the diced tomatoes and chicken broth, and bring the mixture to a simmer.
Stir in the chili powder, ground cumin, paprika, salt, and pepper.
Add the cooked and shredded chicken to the pot and let the soup simmer for 10-15 minutes to allow the flavors to meld together.
Taste the soup and adjust the seasonings as needed.
Stir in the chopped fresh cilantro and the lime juice just before serving.
Serve the Keto Chicken Tortilla Soup hot, garnished with your favorite keto-friendly toppings, such as sliced avocado, shredded cheese, sour cream, chopped green onions, and crushed pork rinds or low-carb tortilla chips for added crunch.
This Keto Chicken Tortilla Soup is rich and flavorful, without the traditional high-carb ingredients. It's a perfect choice for those following a low-carb or keto diet, and it's also a great way to use up leftover cooked chicken. Enjoy the delicious taste of this comforting soup while staying within your carb limits!

Keto Cream Of Asparagus Soup

Ingredients:

1 lb asparagus, tough ends trimmed and chopped into small pieces
1 small onion, chopped
2 cloves garlic, minced
2 tablespoons butter
4 cups chicken or vegetable broth
1 cup heavy cream
Salt and pepper to taste
Optional toppings: grated Parmesan cheese, crispy bacon bits, chopped fresh chives or parsley

Instructions:

In a large pot or Dutch oven, melt the butter over medium heat.
Add the chopped onion and minced garlic to the pot. Sauté until the onion becomes translucent and the garlic becomes fragrant, about 2-3 minutes.
Add the chopped asparagus to the pot and continue to sauté for another 2 minutes.
Pour in the chicken or vegetable broth, and bring the mixture to a simmer.
Cover the pot and let the asparagus cook in the broth until tender, about 10-15 minutes.
Using an immersion blender or regular blender, carefully puree the soup until smooth.
Return the pureed soup to the pot and stir in the heavy cream.
Let the soup simmer for a few more minutes, allowing the flavors to come together.
Season the soup with salt and pepper to your taste preference.
Serve the Keto Cream of Asparagus Soup hot, garnished with grated Parmesan cheese, crispy bacon bits, and chopped fresh chives or parsley for added flavor and texture.
This Keto Cream of Asparagus Soup is creamy and satisfying, while being low in carbs and packed with nutritious asparagus. It's a great way to enjoy a comforting soup without compromising your keto lifestyle. Enjoy the delicious taste and goodness of this keto-friendly asparagus soup!

Keto Cream Of Mushroom Soup

Ingredients:

1 lb mushrooms (cremini or white button), sliced
1 small onion, diced
2 cloves garlic, minced
2 tablespoons butter
4 cups chicken or vegetable broth
1 cup heavy cream
1/4 cup grated Parmesan cheese
Salt and pepper to taste
Optional: Fresh thyme or parsley for garnish

Instructions:

In a large pot or Dutch oven, melt the butter over medium heat.
Add the diced onion and minced garlic to the pot. Sauté until the onion becomes translucent and the garlic becomes fragrant, about 2-3 minutes.
Add the sliced mushrooms to the pot and continue to sauté until they release their moisture and become tender, about 5-7 minutes.
Pour in the chicken or vegetable broth, and bring the mixture to a simmer.
Cover the pot and let the mushrooms cook in the broth for another 10 minutes.
Using an immersion blender or regular blender, carefully puree about half of the soup until smooth. This step helps create a creamy texture while still leaving some mushroom pieces for added texture.
Return the pureed soup to the pot and stir in the heavy cream and grated Parmesan cheese.
Let the soup simmer for a few more minutes, allowing the flavors to meld together.
Season the soup with salt and pepper to your taste preference.
Serve the Keto Cream of Mushroom Soup hot, garnished with fresh thyme or parsley for added aroma and presentation.
This Keto Cream of Mushroom Soup is rich, creamy, and full of earthy mushroom flavor. It's a perfect comfort food for those following a low-carb or keto diet, and it's easy to make with simple ingredients. Enjoy this delicious and satisfying soup as a warm and nourishing meal!

Hungarian low carb Goulash

Ingredients:

1.5 lbs beef stew meat, cut into cubes
2 tablespoons olive oil
1 large onion, diced
2 cloves garlic, minced
2 tablespoons sweet paprika
1 teaspoon smoked paprika (optional, for a smoky flavor)
1 teaspoon caraway seeds
1 red bell pepper, diced
1 green bell pepper, diced
1 can (14 oz) diced tomatoes
2 cups beef broth
Salt and pepper to taste
Fresh parsley, chopped, for garnish

nstructions:

In a large pot or Dutch oven, heat the olive oil over medium-high heat.
Add the diced onions and sauté until they become translucent, about 2-3 minutes
Add the minced garlic and sauté for another 1 minute until fragrant.
Add the beef cubes to the pot and cook until they are browned on all sides.
Stir in the sweet paprika, smoked paprika (if using), and caraway seeds, coating the meat and onions with the spices.
Add the diced red and green bell peppers to the pot and cook for 2-3 minutes until they start to soften.
Pour in the diced tomatoes and beef broth, and bring the mixture to a simmer.
Reduce the heat to low, cover the pot, and let the Goulash simmer for about 1.5 to 2 hours, or until the meat becomes tender and flavors meld together. Stir occasionally.
Taste the Goulash and season with salt and pepper according to your preference.
Serve the Hungarian low-carb Goulash hot, garnished with chopped fresh parsley.
This low-carb Hungarian Goulash is rich and flavorful, without the high-carb ingredients. It's a hearty and comforting dish that's perfect for a satisfying low-carb meal. Enjoy the traditional taste of Goulash while staying within your low-carb diet!

Low Carb Sausage Stew

Ingredients:

1 lb low-carb sausages (such as chicken, turkey, or pork sausages), sliced
2 tablespoons olive oil
1 onion, diced
2 cloves garlic, minced
2 celery stalks, chopped
2 carrots, peeled and chopped
1 bell pepper (any color), diced
1 can (14 oz) diced tomatoes
4 cups chicken or vegetable broth
1 teaspoon dried thyme
1 teaspoon dried oregano
1 bay leaf
Salt and pepper to taste
Optional: chopped fresh parsley or basil for garnish

Instructions:

In a large pot or Dutch oven, heat the olive oil over medium heat.

Add the sliced sausages to the pot and cook until they are browned on all sides. Remove the sausages from the pot and set them aside.
In the same pot, add the diced onions and sauté until they become translucent, about 2-3 minutes.
Add the minced garlic, chopped celery, chopped carrots, and diced bell pepper to the pot. Sauté for another 2-3 minutes until the vegetables start to soften.
Pour in the diced tomatoes and chicken or vegetable broth, and bring the mixture to a simmer.
Stir in the dried thyme, dried oregano, bay leaf, and cooked sausages.
Reduce the heat to low, cover the pot, and let the stew simmer for about 20-25 minutes, or until the vegetables are tender and the flavors meld together.
Taste the stew and season with salt and pepper according to your preference.
Optional: Garnish the Low Carb Sausage Stew with chopped fresh parsley or basil before serving.
Serve the Low Carb Sausage Stew hot and enjoy a comforting and hearty low-carb meal!
This Low Carb Sausage Stew is packed with protein from the sausages and loaded with nutritious vegetables. It's a satisfying and flavorful option for anyone looking to maintain a low-carb lifestyle. Enjoy this delicious and comforting stew while staying on track with your low-carb diet!

Creamy Keto Cauliflower Soup

Ingredients:

1 medium head of cauliflower, chopped into florets
2 tablespoons butter
1 small onion, diced
2 cloves garlic, minced
4 cups chicken or vegetable broth
1 cup heavy cream
1/4 cup grated Parmesan cheese
Salt and pepper to taste
Optional toppings: crispy bacon bits, chopped chives, shredded cheese

Instructions:

In a large pot or Dutch oven, melt the butter over medium heat.
Add the diced onion and minced garlic to the pot. Sauté until the onion becomes translucent and the garlic becomes fragrant, about 2-3 minutes.
Add the chopped cauliflower florets to the pot and sauté for another 2-3 minutes.
Pour in the chicken or vegetable broth, and bring the mixture to a simmer.
Cover the pot and let the cauliflower cook in the broth until it becomes tender, about 10-15 minutes.
Using an immersion blender or regular blender, carefully puree the soup until smooth and creamy.
Return the pureed soup to the pot and stir in the heavy cream and grated Parmesan cheese.
Let the soup simmer for a few more minutes, allowing the flavors to meld together.
Season the soup with salt and pepper to your taste preference.
Serve the Creamy Keto Cauliflower Soup hot, garnished with optional toppings like crispy bacon bits, chopped chives, or shredded cheese for added flavor and texture.
This Creamy Keto Cauliflower Soup is rich, velvety, and satisfying, without the high carbs typically found in traditional creamy soups. It's a perfect choice for those following a low-carb or keto diet, and it's easy to make with simple ingredients. Enjoy the luscious taste and creamy texture of this keto-friendly cauliflower soup!

Snack & Sides

BLT Egglets

Ingredients:

6 large eggs
1/4 cup heavy cream
1/2 cup shredded cheddar cheese
4 slices cooked bacon, crumbled
1/4 cup diced tomatoes
1/4 cup chopped lettuce (such as romaine or iceberg)
Salt and pepper to taste
Cooking spray or melted butter for greasing the muffin tin

Instructions:

Preheat your oven to 350°F (175°C) and grease a 6-cup muffin tin with cooking spray or melted butter.
In a mixing bowl, whisk together the eggs and heavy cream until well combined. Stir in the shredded cheddar cheese, crumbled bacon, diced tomatoes, chopped lettuce, salt, and pepper. Mix everything together until the ingredients are evenly distributed.
Pour the egg mixture into the greased muffin tin, dividing it evenly among the 6 cups.
Bake the BLT Egglets in the preheated oven for about 15-18 minutes or until they are set and lightly golden on top.
Remove the Egglets from the oven and let them cool in the muffin tin for a few minutes.
Carefully remove the BLT Egglets from the muffin tin and serve them warm.
These BLT Egglets make a perfect low-carb snack or breakfast option. They are loaded with the delicious flavors of bacon, lettuce, and tomatoes, all wrapped up in a convenient and portable form. Enjoy these tasty and protein-rich treats as a satisfying low-carb snack!

Keto Snickers Bar

Ingredients:

For the nougat layer:

1/2 cup almond flour
2 tablespoons powdered erythritol or your preferred keto sweetener
2 tablespoons unsalted butter, melted
1/2 teaspoon vanilla extract
1 tablespoon heavy cream

For the caramel layer:
1/4 cup sugar-free caramel sauce (store-bought or homemade)
For the peanut layer:
1/2 cup roasted unsalted peanuts
For the chocolate coating:
1/2 cup sugar-free dark chocolate chips or chopped dark chocolate
1 tablespoon coconut oil

Instructions:

In a mixing bowl, combine the almond flour, powdered erythritol, melted butter, vanilla extract, and heavy cream to make the nougat layer. Mix until well combined.
Line a small rectangular or square container with parchment paper or plastic wrap. Press the nougat mixture evenly into the bottom of the container.
Pour the sugar-free caramel sauce over the nougat layer, spreading it out evenly.
Sprinkle the roasted peanuts over the caramel layer, pressing them gently into the caramel.
Place the container in the freezer for about 30 minutes to set the layers.
In the meantime, prepare the chocolate coating. In a microwave-safe bowl, melt the sugar-free dark chocolate chips or chopped dark chocolate with the coconut oil in 30-second intervals, stirring in between, until smooth.
Remove the container from the freezer. Using the parchment paper or plastic wrap, lift the layered mixture from the container and place it on a cutting board.
Cut the mixture into small bar-sized pieces.
Dip each bar into the melted chocolate, coating all sides evenly. Place the coated bars on a parchment-lined tray
Place the tray in the refrigerator for about 10-15 minutes to set the chocolate coating.
Once the chocolate is set, your homemade keto Snickers Bars are ready to enjoy! Store any leftovers in the refrigerator.
These keto Snickers Bars are a delicious and satisfying treat for those following a low-carb lifestyle. They have the perfect combination of nougat, caramel, peanuts, and chocolate, just like the classic Snickers, but without the high carb content. Enjoy these guilt-free and tasty treats!

Air Fryer Loaded Zucchini Skins

Ingredients:

3 medium zucchinis
1 tablespoon olive oil
1/2 cup shredded cheddar cheese
1/4 cup cooked and crumbled bacon
2 tablespoons chopped green onions
Salt and pepper to taste
Sour cream or Greek yogurt for dipping (optional)

Instructions:

Preheat your air fryer to 375°F (190°C).
Cut each zucchini in half lengthwise, and then scoop out the seeds and center pulp, leaving about 1/4 inch of zucchini flesh to create "zucchini boats."
Brush the inside and outside of the zucchini boats with olive oil, and season with salt and pepper.
Place the zucchini boats in the air fryer basket, skin side down.
Air fry the zucchini boats for about 5-6 minutes, or until they are slightly softened.
Remove the zucchini boats from the air fryer, and carefully flip them over, so the scooped side is facing up.
Fill each zucchini boat with shredded cheddar cheese, crumbled bacon, and chopped green onions.
Place the filled zucchini boats back in the air fryer and air fry for another 4-5 minutes, or until the cheese is melted and bubbly.
Remove the loaded zucchini skins from the air fryer and let them cool slightly.
Serve the Air Fryer Loaded Zucchini Skins with sour cream or Greek yogurt for dipping if desired.
These Air Fryer Loaded Zucchini Skins are a delicious and nutritious low-carb snack or appetizer. They are packed with flavor from the cheesy and bacon-filled centers, making them a perfect option for anyone following a low-carb or keto lifestyle. Enjoy these zucchini skins as a healthier alternative to traditional loaded potato skins!

Magic Keto Cookies

Magic Keto Cookies, also known as "Keto Almond Flour Cookies" or "Keto Magic Cookie Bars," are a delightful and easy-to-make dessert that fits well into a low-carb or keto diet. They are reminiscent of the popular "Magic Cookie Bars" but with low-carb ingredients. Here's the recipe:

ngredients:

1 1/2 cups almond flour
1/4 cup unsweetened shredded coconut
1/4 cup sugar-free chocolate chips
1/4 cup chopped nuts (such as pecans or walnuts)
1/4 cup unsalted butter, melted
1/4 cup keto-friendly sweetener (such as erythritol or stevia)
1 teaspoon vanilla extract
Pinch of salt

Instructions:

Preheat your oven to 350°F (175°C) and line a baking sheet with parchment paper.
In a mixing bowl, combine the almond flour, shredded coconut, sugar-free chocolate chips, chopped nuts, keto-friendly sweetener, vanilla extract, and a pinch of salt. Mix well until all the ingredients are evenly distributed.

Pour in the melted unsalted butter and continue to mix until a dough forms.
Take about 1 to 1.5 tablespoons of dough at a time and roll it into balls. Place the dough balls on the prepared baking sheet, leaving some space between them.
Press down lightly on each dough ball to flatten it slightly.
Bake the cookies in the preheated oven for about 12-15 minutes or until they turn golden brown around the edges.
Remove the cookies from the oven and let them cool on the baking sheet for a few minutes.
Transfer the cookies to a wire rack to cool completely.
Once cooled, these Magic Keto Cookies are ready to be enjoyed!
These Magic Keto Cookies are soft, chewy, and full of nutty and chocolatey goodness. They make a perfect treat for satisfying your sweet cravings while keeping your carb intake in check. Enjoy them with a cup of keto-friendly hot beverage or as a guilt-free dessert option!

Keto Rosemary Crackers

Ingredients:

1 cup almond flour
2 tablespoons ground flaxseed meal
1 tablespoon fresh rosemary, finely chopped
1/2 teaspoon garlic powder
1/2 teaspoon onion powder
1/2 teaspoon salt
1 large egg
1 tablespoon olive oil

Instructions:

Preheat your oven to 350°F (175°C) and line a baking sheet with parchment paper.
In a mixing bowl, combine the almond flour, ground flaxseed meal, chopped rosemary, garlic powder, onion powder, and salt. Mix well to evenly distribute the ingredients.
In a separate small bowl, whisk the egg and olive oil together.
Pour the egg-oil mixture into the dry ingredients and mix until it forms a dough.
Place the dough between two sheets of parchment paper and roll it out into a thin layer, about 1/8-inch thick.
Remove the top parchment paper and transfer the rolled-out dough (still on the bottom parchment paper) onto the prepared baking sheet.
Use a pizza cutter or a knife to score the dough into desired cracker shapes and sizes.
Bake the crackers in the preheated oven for about 12-15 minutes or until they turn golden brown and crispy.
Remove the baking sheet from the oven and let the crackers cool on the sheet for a few minutes.
Once cooled, break the crackers apart along the scored lines.
These Keto Rosemary Crackers are flavorful and perfect for dipping into keto-friendly dips or enjoying on their own as a crunchy snack. They are low in carbs and gluten-free, making them an excellent option for those following a low-carb or keto diet. Store any leftovers in an airtight container to keep them fresh for later enjoyment!

Keto Garlic Bread

Ingredients:

1 1/2 cups almond flour
2 tablespoons ground flaxseed meal
1 teaspoon baking powder
1/2 teaspoon garlic powder
1/4 teaspoon salt
2 large eggs
1/4 cup unsalted butter, melted
1/4 cup grated Parmesan cheese
2 cloves garlic, minced
1 tablespoon fresh parsley, chopped (optional, for garnish)

Instructions:

Preheat your oven to 350°F (175°C) and line a loaf pan with parchment paper.
In a mixing bowl, combine the almond flour, ground flaxseed meal, baking powder, garlic powder, and salt. Mix well to evenly distribute the dry ingredients.
In a separate bowl, whisk the eggs and melted butter together.
Pour the egg-butter mixture into the dry ingredients and mix until it forms a thick dough.
Stir in the minced garlic and grated Parmesan cheese, distributing them evenly throughout the dough.
Transfer the dough to the prepared loaf pan and spread it out evenly.
Bake the Keto Garlic Bread in the preheated oven for about 25-30 minutes or until it turns golden brown and a toothpick inserted into the center comes out clean.
Remove the bread from the oven and let it cool slightly in the pan.
Once cooled, remove the bread from the pan using the parchment paper and let it cool completely on a wire rack.
Optionally, sprinkle chopped fresh parsley on top of the bread for added flavor and presentation.
Slice the Keto Garlic Bread into pieces and serve it warm or at room temperature. It's a flavorful and satisfying alternative to traditional garlic bread, without the high carb content. Enjoy it as a side dish, with keto-friendly soups and stews, or as a delicious snack on its own!

Peanut Butter Chocolate Fat Bombs

Ingredients:

1/2 cup creamy peanut butter (unsweetened and with no added sugar)
4 tablespoons coconut oil, melted
2 tablespoons unsweetened cocoa powder
2 tablespoons powdered erythritol or your preferred keto sweetener (adjust to taste)
1/2 teaspoon vanilla extract
Pinch of salt

Instructions:

In a microwave-safe bowl, melt the coconut oil until it's in liquid form.
Add the creamy peanut butter to the melted coconut oil, and mix well until smooth.
Stir in the unsweetened cocoa powder, powdered erythritol, vanilla extract, and a pinch of salt. Mix until all the ingredients are fully combined and the mixture is smooth.
Taste the mixture and adjust the sweetness to your preference by adding more sweetener if needed.
Pour the peanut butter chocolate mixture into silicone candy molds, mini cupcake liners, or an ice cube tray. This will help create bite-sized fat bomb servings.
Place the molds or tray in the refrigerator for about 1-2 hours, or until the fat bombs are firm and set.
Once the fat bombs are fully set, remove them from the molds or liners and store them in an airtight container in the refrigerator.
Enjoy these Peanut Butter Chocolate Fat Bombs as a tasty and satisfying low-carb treat. They are rich in healthy fats and perfect for those following a ketogenic or low-carb diet. These fat bombs can help curb cravings and provide a quick energy boost throughout the day!

Zucchini Pizza Bites

Ingredients:

2 medium zucchinis, sliced into rounds (about 1/4-inch thick)
1/2 cup sugar-free marinara sauce or pizza sauce
1 cup shredded mozzarella cheese
1/4 cup grated Parmesan cheese
Your favorite pizza toppings (e.g., pepperoni slices, sliced olives, bell peppers, etc.)
Olive oil
Dried oregano or Italian seasoning (optional, for extra flavor)

Instructions:

Preheat your oven to 425°F (220°C) and line a baking sheet with parchment paper.
Lay the zucchini rounds on the prepared baking sheet in a single layer. Lightly brush the tops with olive oil.
Bake the zucchini rounds in the preheated oven for about 5 minutes to soften them slightly.
Remove the baking sheet from the oven and spread a thin layer of sugar-free marinara or pizza sauce on top of each zucchini round.
Sprinkle shredded mozzarella cheese and grated Parmesan cheese over the sauce.
Add your favorite pizza toppings on each zucchini round. Get creative with your toppings!
Sprinkle a pinch of dried oregano or Italian seasoning over the pizza bites for added flavor (optional).
Place the baking sheet back in the oven and bake for another 8-10 minutes, or until the cheese is melted and bubbly.
Remove the Zucchini Pizza Bites from the oven and let them cool slightly before serving.
These Zucchini Pizza Bites are a fantastic low-carb alternative to traditional pizza. They are perfect as an appetizer, party snack, or even a light lunch or dinner. Enjoy the delicious taste of pizza while getting the benefits of zucchini's low carb content and nutrients!

Cauliflower Tots

Ingredients:

1 medium head of cauliflower
1 large egg
1/2 cup almond flour
1/2 cup grated Parmesan cheese
2 tablespoons chopped fresh parsley (or your preferred herbs)
1 teaspoon garlic powder
1/2 teaspoon onion powder
Salt and pepper to taste
Cooking spray or olive oil, for greasing

Instructions:

Preheat your oven to 400°F (200°C) and line a baking sheet with parchment paper. Grease the parchment paper with cooking spray or a drizzle of olive oil to prevent sticking.
Cut the cauliflower into florets and place them in a food processor. Pulse until the cauliflower is finely chopped and resembles rice.
Transfer the cauliflower rice to a microwave-safe bowl and microwave on high for about 5 minutes. This helps soften the cauliflower.
Once the cauliflower is done microwaving, allow it to cool slightly. Then, place it in a clean kitchen towel or cheesecloth and squeeze out as much excess moisture as possible. This step is essential to achieve crispy tots.
In a large mixing bowl, combine the drained cauliflower, egg, almond flour, grated Parmesan cheese, chopped parsley, garlic powder, onion powder, salt, and pepper. Mix until well combined and a dough-like consistency forms.
Take about 1 tablespoon of the cauliflower mixture at a time and roll it into a small tot shape. Place the tots on the prepared baking sheet, leaving some space between each one.
Bake the Cauliflower Tots in the preheated oven for about 20-25 minutes, or until they turn golden brown and crispy.
Remove the tots from the oven and let them cool slightly before serving.
These Cauliflower Tots are a wonderful low-carb alternative to traditional potato tots. They are crispy on the outside and tender on the inside, making them a perfect snack or appetizer for anyone following a low-carb or keto diet. Enjoy them on their own or with your favorite dipping sauce!

Keto Tortilla Chips

Ingredients:

1 cup shredded mozzarella cheese
1/2 cup almond flour
1 teaspoon ground flaxseed meal (optional, for added crunch)
1/2 teaspoon garlic powder
1/2 teaspoon onion powder
1/2 teaspoon paprika
Pinch of salt
Cooking spray or olive oil, for greasing

Instructions:

Preheat your oven to 400°F (200°C) and line a baking sheet with parchment paper. Grease the parchment paper with cooking spray or a drizzle of olive oil to prevent sticking.
In a microwave-safe bowl, melt the shredded mozzarella cheese in the microwave until fully melted and gooey.
In a separate mixing bowl, combine the almond flour, ground flaxseed meal (if using), garlic powder, onion powder, paprika, and a pinch of salt.
Add the melted mozzarella cheese to the dry ingredients and mix until it forms a dough.
Place the dough between two sheets of parchment paper and roll it out into a thin, even layer.
Use a pizza cutter or a knife to cut the rolled-out dough into triangle-shaped chips or any desired shape.
Carefully transfer the cut chips to the prepared baking sheet.
Bake the Keto Tortilla Chips in the preheated oven for about 10-12 minutes, or until they turn golden brown and crispy.
Remove the chips from the oven and let them cool on the baking sheet for a few minutes. They will become even crispier as they cool.
Enjoy these homemade Keto Tortilla Chips as a crunchy and satisfying snack! They are perfect for dipping in guacamole, salsa, or your favorite keto-friendly dips. These chips are low in carbs and high in flavor, making them a fantastic alternative to traditional tortilla chips for those following a ketogenic or low-carb lifestyle.

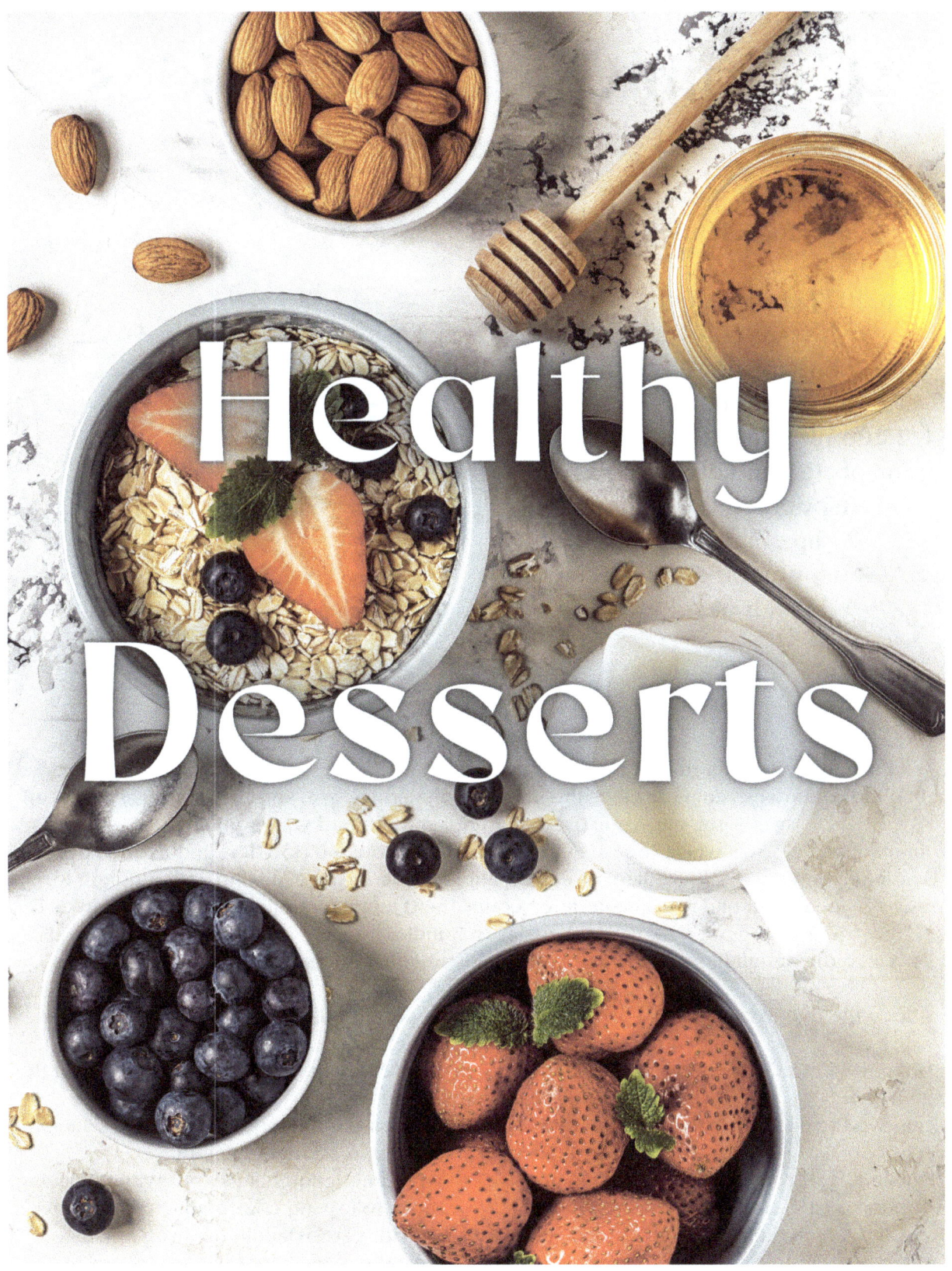

Cream Cheese Cookies

Ingredients:

4 oz (1/2 cup) cream cheese, softened
1/2 cup unsalted butter, softened
1/2 cup powdered erythritol or your preferred keto sweetener
1 teaspoon vanilla extract
2 cups almond flour
1/2 teaspoon baking powder
Pinch of salt

Instructions:

Preheat your oven to 350°F (175°C) and line a baking sheet with parchment paper.
In a mixing bowl, cream together the softened cream cheese, softened butter, powdered erythritol, and vanilla extract until smooth and well combined.
In a separate bowl, whisk together the almond flour, baking powder, and a pinch of salt.
Gradually add the dry ingredients to the cream cheese mixture, mixing until a dough forms.
Cover the dough and refrigerate it for about 15-30 minutes. Chilling the dough makes it easier to handle.
Once the dough has chilled, use your hands to roll it into small balls, about 1 inch in diameter.
Place the dough balls on the prepared baking sheet and gently press down on each one with a fork to create a criss-cross pattern.
Bake the Keto Cream Cheese Cookies in the preheated oven for 12-15 minutes, or until the edges turn golden brown.
Remove the cookies from the oven and let them cool on the baking sheet for a few minutes before transferring them to a wire rack to cool completely.
These Keto Cream Cheese Cookies are soft, chewy, and delightfully sweet with a creamy texture. They are low in carbs and perfect for those following a ketogenic or low-carb diet. Enjoy them as a sweet treat with your favorite keto-friendly beverage or as a satisfying dessert option!

Cheesecake

Ingredients:

For the crust:

1 1/2 cups almond flour
1/4 cup powdered erythritol or your preferred keto sweetener
1/3 cup unsalted butter, melted

For the filling:

24 oz (three 8-ounce packages) cream cheese, softened
3/4 cup powdered erythritol or your preferred keto sweetener
3 large eggs
1 teaspoon vanilla extract
1/4 cup heavy cream

Instructions:

Preheat your oven to 325°F (160°C). Grease a 9-inch springform pan with butter or cooking spray.
In a mixing bowl, combine the almond flour, powdered erythritol, and melted unsalted butter to make the crust. Mix until the ingredients are well combined and the mixture resembles wet sand.
Press the crust mixture evenly into the bottom of the prepared springform pan to form the cheesecake crust.
In a large mixing bowl, beat the softened cream cheese and powdered erythritol together until smooth and creamy.
Add the eggs, one at a time, to the cream cheese mixture, mixing well after each addition.
Stir in the vanilla extract and heavy cream until the filling is smooth and well combined.
Pour the filling over the crust in the springform pan, spreading it out evenly.
Place the cheesecake in the preheated oven and bake for about 45-55 minutes, or until the edges are set, and the center is slightly jiggly.
Turn off the oven and leave the cheesecake inside for another hour to cool gradually.
Remove the cheesecake from the oven and let it cool completely at room temperature.
Cover the cooled cheesecake with plastic wrap and refrigerate it for at least 4 hours (preferably overnight) to set.

Blueberry Muffins

Ingredients:

2 cups almond flour
1/4 cup coconut flour
1/3 cup powdered erythritol or your preferred keto sweetener
1 teaspoon baking powder
1/4 teaspoon baking soda
Pinch of salt
3 large eggs
1/2 cup unsweetened almond milk (or any other keto-friendly milk)
1/4 cup melted coconut oil or unsalted butter
1 teaspoon vanilla extract
1 cup fresh blueberries

Instructions:

Preheat your oven to 350°F (175°C). Line a muffin tin with paper liners or grease the muffin cups with cooking spray.
In a large mixing bowl, whisk together the almond flour, coconut flour, powdered erythritol, baking powder, baking soda, and a pinch of salt.
In a separate bowl, beat the eggs, almond milk, melted coconut oil (or butter), and vanilla extract until well combined.
Pour the wet ingredients into the dry ingredients and stir until a thick batter forms.
Gently fold in the fresh blueberries into the batter.
Divide the batter evenly among the prepared muffin cups, filling each one about 2/3 full.
Bake the Blueberry Muffins in the preheated oven for 20-25 minutes or until a toothpick inserted into the center of a muffin comes out clean.
Remove the muffins from the oven and let them cool in the muffin tin for a few minutes before transferring them to a wire rack to cool completely.
Enjoy these delicious and moist Blueberry Muffins as a satisfying breakfast or snack option on a low-carb or keto diet. They are bursting with juicy blueberries and have a delightful muffin texture, making them a perfect treat for anyone watching their carb intake!

Ice Cream

Ingredients:

2 cups heavy cream
1 cup unsweetened almond milk or coconut milk
1/2 cup powdered erythritol or your preferred keto sweetener
1 teaspoon vanilla extract
Pinch of salt
4 large egg yolks
Optional: sugar-free chocolate chips, nuts, or other keto-friendly mix-ins

Instructions:

In a saucepan, combine the heavy cream, almond milk (or coconut milk), powdered erythritol, vanilla extract, and a pinch of salt. Heat the mixture over medium-low heat until it's hot but not boiling. Stir occasionally to dissolve the sweetener.
In a separate bowl, whisk the egg yolks.
Gradually add a small amount of the hot cream mixture into the whisked egg yolks while continuously whisking. This is to temper the yolks and avoid scrambling them.
Slowly pour the tempered egg yolk mixture back into the saucepan with the rest of the hot cream mixture, stirring constantly.
Continue cooking the mixture over low heat, stirring constantly, until it thickens and coats the back of a spoon. This should take about 5-7 minutes.
Remove the saucepan from the heat and let the ice cream base cool to room temperature.
Once cooled, cover the saucepan with plastic wrap, ensuring the wrap touches the surface of the ice cream base to prevent a skin from forming. Refrigerate the mixture for at least 4 hours or preferably overnight.
After chilling, pour the ice cream base into an ice cream maker and churn it according to the manufacturer's instructions. If you don't have an ice cream maker, you can place the mixture in the freezer and whisk it every 30 minutes for the first few hours until it reaches the desired consistency.
Optional: During the last few minutes of churning or mixing, add sugar-free chocolate chips, nuts, or any other keto-friendly mix-ins you desire.
Transfer the churned ice cream to a lidded container and freeze for an additional 2-4 hours, or until firm.
Now you have a creamy and satisfying Keto Ice Cream to enjoy as a delicious treat while keeping your carb intake in check. Feel free to experiment with different flavors and mix-ins to create your favorite keto ice cream variations!

Keto Chocolate Ice Cream

Ingredients:

2 cups heavy cream
1 cup unsweetened almond milk or coconut milk
1/2 cup powdered erythritol or your preferred keto sweetener
1/2 cup unsweetened cocoa powder
1 teaspoon vanilla extract
Pinch of salt
4 large egg yolks

Instructions:

In a saucepan, combine the heavy cream, almond milk (or coconut milk), powdered erythritol, cocoa powder, vanilla extract, and a pinch of salt. Heat the mixture over medium-low heat until it's hot but not boiling. Stir occasionally to dissolve the sweetener and cocoa powder.
In a separate bowl, whisk the egg yolks.
Gradually add a small amount of the hot cream mixture into the whisked egg yolks while continuously whisking. This is to temper the yolks and avoid scrambling them.
Slowly pour the tempered egg yolk mixture back into the saucepan with the rest of the hot cream mixture, stirring constantly.
Continue cooking the mixture over low heat, stirring constantly, until it thickens and coats the back of a spoon. This should take about 5-7 minutes.
Remove the saucepan from the heat and let the ice cream base cool to room temperature.
Once cooled, cover the saucepan with plastic wrap, ensuring the wrap touches the surface of the ice cream base to prevent a skin from forming. Refrigerate the mixture for at least 4 hours or preferably overnight.
After chilling, pour the ice cream base into an ice cream maker and churn it according to the manufacturer's instructions. If you don't have an ice cream maker, you can place the mixture in the freezer and whisk it every 30 minutes for the first few hours until it reaches the desired consistency.
Transfer the churned ice cream to a lidded container and freeze for an additional 2-4 hours, or until firm.
Now you have a luscious and satisfying Keto Chocolate Ice Cream to indulge in without compromising your low-carb lifestyle. Enjoy this velvety treat on its own or with your favorite keto-friendly toppings like whipped cream, chopped nuts, or sugar-free chocolate sauce!

Pound Cake

Ingredients:

1 1/2 cups almond flour
1/2 cup coconut flour
1 cup unsalted butter, softened
1 cup powdered erythritol or your preferred keto sweetener
4 large eggs
1/2 cup unsweetened almond milk or coconut milk
1 teaspoon vanilla extract
1 teaspoon baking powder
1/4 teaspoon salt
Optional: lemon or orange zest for added flavor

Instructions:

Preheat your oven to 350°F (175°C). Grease a standard-sized loaf pan with butter or cooking spray and line it with parchment paper for easy removal.
In a large mixing bowl, cream together the softened butter and powdered erythritol until light and fluffy.
Add the eggs, one at a time, to the butter mixture, beating well after each addition.
Stir in the vanilla extract and optional lemon or orange zest, if using.
In a separate bowl, whisk together the almond flour, coconut flour, baking powder, and salt.
Gradually add the dry flour mixture to the wet butter mixture, alternating with the unsweetened almond milk (or coconut milk), until a smooth batter forms.
Pour the batter into the prepared loaf pan, spreading it out evenly.
Bake the Low Carb Pound Cake in the preheated oven for about 45-55 minutes or until a toothpick inserted into the center comes out clean.
Remove the pound cake from the oven and let it cool in the pan for about 10 minutes.
Carefully lift the pound cake out of the pan using the parchment paper and transfer it to a wire rack to cool completely.
Slice the Low Carb Pound Cake and serve it as a delicious and satisfying treat for those following a low-carb or keto lifestyle. The pound cake is tender, flavorful, and perfect for enjoying on its own or with a dollop of sugar-free whipped cream and fresh berries. It's a wonderful option for satisfying your sweet cravings while staying on track with your low-carb eating plan!

Almond Flour Pie Crust

Ingredients:

1 1/2 cups almond flour
1/4 cup unsalted butter, melted
1 tablespoon granulated erythritol or your preferred keto sweetener (optional, for a slightly sweet crust)
Pinch of salt

Instructions:

In a mixing bowl, combine the almond flour, melted butter, granulated erythritol (if using), and a pinch of salt.
Stir the ingredients together until they form a crumbly dough that sticks together when pressed with your fingers.
Press the dough evenly into a 9-inch pie dish, covering the bottom and sides. Use your fingers or the back of a spoon to smooth out the crust.
If you are pre-baking the crust for a no-bake filling, refrigerate it for 30 minutes before baking. This helps the crust hold its shape.
Preheat your oven to 350°F (175°C).
If you are using the crust for a baked pie filling, follow the recipe instructions for baking the entire pie with the filling. Otherwise, if pre-baking, place the pie crust in the preheated oven and bake for 10-12 minutes, or until it turns golden brown.
Once the crust is baked or pre-baked, remove it from the oven and let it cool completely before filling it with your desired pie filling.
This almond flour pie crust is not only low-carb and gluten-free but also adds a delicious nutty flavor to your favorite pies. Whether you're making a classic fruit pie or a custard-based pie, this almond flour crust will be a perfect and keto-friendly base for your creations! Enjoy your homemade pies without the guilt!

Keto Coconut Cream Pie

Almond Flour Pie Crust:

Ingredients:

1 1/2 cups almond flour
1/4 cup unsalted butter, melted
1 tablespoon granulated erythritol or your preferred keto sweetener (optional, for a slightly sweet crust)
Pinch of salt

Keto Coconut Cream Pie Filling:

Ingredients:

1 1/2 cups unsweetened coconut milk
1/2 cup heavy cream
1/2 cup powdered erythritol or your preferred keto sweetener
4 large egg yolks
2 tablespoons coconut flour
1/2 cup unsweetened shredded coconut
2 tablespoons unsalted butter
1 teaspoon vanilla extract
Whipped cream and toasted coconut, for garnish (optional)

Instructions:

In a mixing bowl, combine the almond flour, melted butter, granulated erythritol (if using), and a pinch of salt.
Stir the ingredients together until they form a crumbly dough that sticks together when pressed with your fingers.
Press the dough evenly into a 9-inch pie dish, covering the bottom and sides. Use your fingers or the back of a spoon to smooth out the crust.
Preheat your oven to 350°F (175°C).
Place the pie crust in the preheated oven and bake for 10-12 minutes, or until it turns golden brown. Remove it from the oven and let it cool completely before filling.

Instructions:

In a saucepan, combine the coconut milk, heavy cream, and powdered erythritol over medium heat. Stir until the sweetener dissolves, and the mixture is hot but not boiling.
In a separate bowl, whisk the egg yolks. Slowly add a small amount of the hot cream mixture into the egg yolks while continuously whisking. This is to temper the yolks and avoid scrambling them.
Gradually pour the tempered egg yolk mixture back into the saucepan with the rest of the hot cream mixture, stirring constantly.
Add the coconut flour and continue to cook the filling over medium heat, stirring constantly until it thickens to a pudding-like consistency.
Remove the saucepan from the heat and stir in the shredded coconut, unsalted butter, and vanilla extract until well combined.
Pour the coconut cream filling into the cooled almond flour pie crust, spreading it out evenly.
Cover the pie with plastic wrap, ensuring it touches the surface of the filling to prevent a skin from forming. Refrigerate the pie for at least 4 hours or preferably overnight to set.

Optionally, garnish the pie with whipped cream and toasted coconut before serving.
This Keto Coconut Cream Pie is a delightful and satisfying dessert for anyone following a low-carb or keto lifestyle. The creamy coconut filling paired with the almond flour crust creates a delicious pie that's perfect for special occasions or any time you want a sweet treat! Enjoy!

Healthy Zucchini Muffins

Ingredients:

1 1/2 cups almond flour
1/4 cup coconut flour
1/2 teaspoon baking soda
1/2 teaspoon baking powder
1/2 teaspoon ground cinnamon
1/4 teaspoon salt
3 large eggs
1/4 cup melted coconut oil or unsalted butter
1/4 cup unsweetened applesauce
1/4 cup powdered erythritol or your preferred keto sweetener
1 teaspoon vanilla extract
1 cup shredded zucchini (excess moisture squeezed out)
1/4 cup chopped walnuts or pecans (optional, for added crunch)

Instructions:

Preheat your oven to 350°F (175°C). Line a muffin tin with paper liners or grease the muffin cups with cooking spray.
In a large mixing bowl, whisk together the almond flour, coconut flour, baking soda, baking powder, ground cinnamon, and salt.
In a separate bowl, whisk the eggs, melted coconut oil (or butter), unsweetened applesauce, powdered erythritol, and vanilla extract until well combined.
Gradually add the wet ingredients to the dry ingredients, stirring until a smooth batter forms.
Gently fold in the shredded zucchini and chopped nuts (if using) into the batter.
Divide the batter evenly among the prepared muffin cups, filling each one about 2/3 full.
Bake the Healthy Zucchini Muffins in the preheated oven for 18-22 minutes, or until a toothpick inserted into the center of a muffin comes out clean.
Remove the muffins from the oven and let them cool in the muffin tin for a few minutes before transferring them to a wire rack to cool completely.
These Healthy Zucchini Muffins are a great option for a nutritious and low-carb breakfast or snack. They are moist, flavorful, and packed with wholesome ingredients like zucchini and almond flour. Enjoy them warm or at room temperature, and store any leftovers in an airtight container for later enjoyment!

Almond Flour Cake

Ingredients:

2 cups almond flour
1/2 cup granulated erythritol or your preferred keto sweetener
1/2 teaspoon baking powder
Pinch of salt
4 large eggs
1/2 cup unsalted butter, melted
1/2 cup unsweetened almond milk or coconut milk
1 teaspoon vanilla extract

Instructions:

Preheat your oven to 350°F (175°C). Grease a 9-inch round cake pan or line it with parchment paper for easy removal.
In a large mixing bowl, whisk together the almond flour, granulated erythritol, baking powder, and a pinch of salt.
In a separate bowl, whisk the eggs, melted butter, almond milk (or coconut milk), and vanilla extract until well combined.
Gradually add the wet ingredients to the dry ingredients, stirring until a smooth batter forms.
Pour the cake batter into the prepared cake pan, spreading it out evenly.
Bake the Almond Flour Cake in the preheated oven for 25-30 minutes, or until a toothpick inserted into the center comes out clean.
Remove the cake from the oven and let it cool in the pan for about 10 minutes. Carefully transfer the cake to a wire rack to cool completely.
You can enjoy this Low Carb Almond Flour Cake as is, or top it with your favorite keto-friendly frosting or a dusting of powdered erythritol for extra sweetness. It's a wonderfully moist and tender cake with a delightful nutty flavor from the almond flour. Perfect for any occasion or as a satisfying treat for those following a low-carb or keto lifestyle!

Keto Brownies (Almond Flour)

Ingredients:

1 cup almond flour
1/2 cup unsweetened cocoa powder
1/2 cup granulated erythritol or your preferred keto sweetener
1/2 cup unsalted butter, melted
2 large eggs
1 teaspoon vanilla extract
1/4 teaspoon salt
Optional: 1/4 cup chopped sugar-free chocolate or sugar-free chocolate chips

Instructions:

Preheat your oven to 350°F (175°C). Grease or line an 8x8 inch (20x20 cm) square baking pan with parchment paper.
In a mixing bowl, whisk together the almond flour, cocoa powder, granulated erythritol, and salt until well combined.
In a separate bowl, whisk the melted butter, eggs, and vanilla extract until smooth.
Gradually add the wet ingredients to the dry ingredients, stirring until a thick and smooth batter forms.
If desired, fold in the chopped sugar-free chocolate or sugar-free chocolate chips for extra richness and texture.
Pour the batter into the prepared baking pan, spreading it out evenly.
Bake the Keto Brownies in the preheated oven for 20-25 minutes, or until a toothpick inserted into the center comes out with moist crumbs (not wet batter).
Remove the brownies from the oven and let them cool in the pan for about 15-20 minutes. Carefully lift the brownies out of the pan using the parchment paper and transfer them to a wire rack to cool completely.
Once the Keto Brownies have cooled, you can cut them into squares and enjoy these delectable and guilt-free treats! These brownies are rich, chocolatey, and perfectly low-carb, making them an excellent option for satisfying your sweet cravings while following a keto or low-carb lifestyle. Enjoy them with a cup of coffee or as a delightful dessert!

Keto Seafood Gratin

Ingredients:

1 lb mixed seafood (such as shrimp, scallops, and crab meat), cooked and drained
1 tablespoon olive oil
2 tablespoons unsalted butter
1 small onion, finely chopped
2 cloves garlic, minced
1 cup heavy cream
1/2 cup chicken or seafood broth
1/4 cup grated Parmesan cheese
1/4 cup shredded mozzarella cheese
1/4 cup chopped fresh parsley
1/2 teaspoon dried thyme
Salt and pepper to taste
1/4 cup almond flour
Optional: 1/4 cup crushed pork rinds (for added crunch)

Instructions:

Preheat your oven to 375°F (190°C). Grease a baking dish with butter or cooking spray.
In a large skillet, heat the olive oil over medium heat. Add the chopped onion and minced garlic, and sauté until they become translucent and fragrant.
Add the cooked seafood to the skillet and stir to combine with the onions and garlic. Season with salt and pepper to taste.
In a separate saucepan, melt the unsalted butter over medium heat. Stir in the heavy cream and chicken or seafood broth. Bring the mixture to a gentle simmer.
Reduce the heat to low and gradually add the grated Parmesan cheese and shredded mozzarella cheese to the cream mixture, stirring until the cheese melts and the sauce becomes smooth.
Stir in the chopped fresh parsley and dried thyme, and season the sauce with salt and pepper to taste.
Pour the creamy sauce over the seafood mixture in the skillet and stir to coat the seafood evenly.
Transfer the seafood and sauce mixture to the greased baking dish.
In a small bowl, combine the almond flour with optional crushed pork rinds for added crunch. Sprinkle this mixture evenly over the top of the seafood mixture in the baking dish.
Bake the Keto Seafood Gratin in the preheated oven for 15-20 minutes, or until the top is golden and bubbly.
Remove the gratin from the oven and let it cool for a few minutes before serving.
Enjoy this rich and comforting Keto Seafood Gratin as a satisfying and elegant dish that's low in carbs and high in flavor! It's perfect for special occasions or a hearty weeknight dinner while staying on track with your keto or low-carb lifestyle.

Lobster Bisque

Ingredients:

2 lobster tails (about 8 oz each), shells removed and chopped into chunks
2 tablespoons unsalted butter
1 small onion, finely chopped
2 cloves garlic, minced
2 cups seafood or chicken broth
1 cup heavy cream
1/4 cup dry white wine (optional)
1 tablespoon tomato paste
1 teaspoon paprika
1/2 teaspoon dried thyme
Pinch of cayenne pepper (optional, for a bit of heat)
Salt and pepper to taste
Chopped fresh parsley, for garnish

Instructions:

In a large saucepan or soup pot, melt the unsalted butter over medium heat.
Add the chopped onion and minced garlic to the melted butter and sauté until the onion becomes translucent and fragrant.
Add the chopped lobster tail pieces to the saucepan and cook for a few minutes until they start to turn opaque.
Pour in the seafood or chicken broth, and add the dry white wine if using. Bring the mixture to a simmer and let it cook for about 10-15 minutes to infuse the flavors.
Using a slotted spoon, remove the lobster pieces from the pot and set them aside.
Using an immersion blender or regular blender, blend the soup mixture until smooth. Be careful when blending hot liquids, and work in batches if using a regular blender.
Return the blended soup to the pot and stir in the heavy cream, tomato paste, paprika, dried thyme, and cayenne pepper (if using). Season with salt and pepper to taste.
Bring the soup back to a gentle simmer, and add the cooked lobster pieces back to the pot. Let it simmer for a few more minutes to heat through and meld the flavors.
Ladle the Low Carb Lobster Bisque into serving bowls and garnish with chopped fresh parsley.
This rich and flavorful Low Carb Lobster Bisque is a wonderful dish for special occasions or as an indulgent treat while maintaining a low-carb or keto lifestyle. The creamy soup with tender chunks of lobster is sure to impress and delight your taste buds! Enjoy!

Shrimp Boil

Ingredients:

1 lb large shrimp, peeled and deveined
1 lb smoked sausage or kielbasa, cut into slices
1 lb fresh or frozen cauliflower florets
2 ears of corn, husked and cut into chunks (substitute with low-carb vegetables like green beans if desired)
1/2 lb small red potatoes (optional, omit for a lower-carb version)
4 cloves garlic, minced
1 lemon, sliced
4 tablespoons unsalted butter, melted
2 tablespoons Old Bay seasoning (or more to taste)
Salt and pepper to taste
Fresh parsley, chopped (for garnish)

Instructions:

In a large pot, bring water to a boil and add the Old Bay seasoning, salt, and pepper. If you're using potatoes, add them to the pot and cook for about 10 minutes until they start to soften.
Add the cauliflower florets and corn (or green beans) to the pot. Cook for an additional 5-7 minutes until the vegetables are slightly tender.
Add the sliced sausage to the pot and cook for another 5 minutes.
Finally, add the shrimp and minced garlic to the pot. Cook for about 2-3 minutes until the shrimp turn pink and are fully cooked.
Drain the pot, discarding the cooking water.
In a separate small bowl, mix the melted butter and lemon slices.
Pour the butter and lemon mixture over the cooked shrimp, vegetables, and sausage in the pot. Gently toss to coat everything with the flavorful butter.
Transfer the Shrimp Boil to a serving platter or a large bowl.
Garnish with chopped fresh parsley.
This low-carb Shrimp Boil is a fantastic one-pot meal that's bursting with flavors. It's perfect for gatherings or a delightful family dinner. Feel free to customize the ingredients to suit your taste and dietary preferences while still enjoying a delicious and satisfying low-carb dish!

Keto Cioppino

Keto Cioppino is a delightful seafood stew that is perfect for those following a low-carb or keto lifestyle. It is rich, flavorful, and filled with a variety of seafood. Here's a delicious recipe for Keto Cioppino:

Ingredients:

1 lb mixed seafood (such as shrimp, scallops, mussels, and fish fillets), cleaned and cut into bite-sized pieces
2 tablespoons olive oil
1 small onion, finely chopped
2 cloves garlic, minced
1/2 cup dry white wine
1 can (14 oz) crushed tomatoes
2 cups fish or seafood broth
1/2 teaspoon dried oregano
1/2 teaspoon dried thyme
1/4 teaspoon red pepper flakes (adjust to your preferred level of spiciness)
Salt and pepper to taste
2 tablespoons chopped fresh parsley, for garnish

Instructions:

In a large pot or Dutch oven, heat the olive oil over medium heat.
Add the chopped onion and minced garlic to the pot. Sauté until the onion becomes translucent and the garlic is fragrant.
Pour in the dry white wine and let it simmer for a minute or two to cook off the alcohol.
Add the crushed tomatoes, fish or seafood broth, dried oregano, dried thyme, and red pepper flakes to the pot. Stir to combine.
Bring the mixture to a simmer and let it cook for about 15-20 minutes to allow the flavors to meld.
Season the broth with salt and pepper to taste.
Add the mixed seafood to the pot and let it cook for a few minutes until the seafood is fully cooked through. Be careful not to overcook the seafood, as it can become tough.
Once the seafood is cooked, remove the pot from the heat.
Ladle the Keto Cioppino into serving bowls and garnish with chopped fresh parsley.

Low-Carb Keto Shrimp Scampi With Zucchini Noodles

Ingredients:

1 lb large shrimp, peeled and deveined
3 medium zucchini, spiralized or cut into noodles
4 tablespoons unsalted butter
4 cloves garlic, minced
1/4 teaspoon red pepper flakes (adjust to your preferred level of spiciness)
1/4 cup chicken or vegetable broth
1/4 cup dry white wine (optional)
Juice of 1 lemon
Zest of 1 lemon
Salt and pepper to taste
2 tablespoons chopped fresh parsley
Grated Parmesan cheese, for garnish (optional)

Instructions:

Pat the shrimp dry with paper towels and season with salt and pepper.

In a large skillet, melt 2 tablespoons of butter over medium heat.
Add the minced garlic and red pepper flakes to the skillet. Sauté for about 1 minute until the garlic becomes fragrant.
Add the shrimp to the skillet and cook for 2-3 minutes on each side until they turn pink and are fully cooked. Remove the shrimp from the skillet and set them aside.
In the same skillet, add the remaining 2 tablespoons of butter, chicken or vegetable broth, and dry white wine (if using). Let it simmer for a minute or two.
Add the lemon juice and zest to the skillet, and season the sauce with salt and pepper to taste.
Stir in the zucchini noodles and cook for about 2-3 minutes until they are just tender. Be careful not to overcook the zucchini, as it can become too soft.
Return the cooked shrimp to the skillet and toss everything together to coat the zucchini noodles and shrimp with the flavorful sauce.
Remove the skillet from the heat.
Garnish the Shrimp Scampi with chopped fresh parsley and grated Parmesan cheese (if desired).
This Low-Carb Keto Shrimp Scampi with Zucchini Noodles is a light and flavorful dish that's perfect for a quick and satisfying meal. The zucchini noodles make a wonderful substitute for traditional pasta, and the lemony garlic butter sauce enhances the deliciousness of the shrimp. Enjoy this delightful keto-friendly recipe without any guilt!

Keto Garlic Butter Salmon

Ingredients:

4 salmon fillets
2 tablespoons unsalted butter, melted
2 cloves garlic, minced
1 tablespoon fresh lemon juice
1 tablespoon chopped fresh parsley
Salt and pepper to taste
Lemon slices and additional fresh parsley for garnish (optional)

Instructions:

Preheat your oven to 400°F (200°C). Line a baking sheet with parchment paper or lightly grease it with cooking spray.
Place the salmon fillets on the prepared baking sheet.
In a small bowl, mix the melted butter, minced garlic, lemon juice, chopped parsley, salt, and pepper until well combined.
Drizzle the garlic butter mixture evenly over the salmon fillets, making sure to coat them completely.
Bake the salmon in the preheated oven for 12-15 minutes, or until the salmon is cooked through and flakes easily with a fork.
Once the salmon is done baking, remove it from the oven and let it rest for a minute.
Optionally, garnish the Keto Garlic Butter Salmon with lemon slices and additional fresh parsley before serving.
This Keto Garlic Butter Salmon is a delightful and flavorful dish that's perfect for a quick weeknight dinner or a special occasion. The garlic butter sauce adds richness and enhances the natural flavors of the salmon. Serve it with some steamed vegetables or a side salad for a complete and satisfying low-carb meal. Enjoy this healthy and delicious recipe as part of your keto lifestyle!

Low-Carb Shrimp Enchiladas

Ingredients:

For the Enchilada Sauce:

1 can (14 oz) diced tomatoes
1/4 cup chopped onion
2 cloves garlic, minced
1 tablespoon olive oil
1 teaspoon chili powder
1/2 teaspoon ground cumin
1/2 teaspoon dried oregano
Salt and pepper to taste

For the Shrimp Filling:

1 lb large shrimp, peeled and deveined
1 tablespoon olive oil
1/4 cup chopped onion
1/2 red bell pepper, diced
2 cloves garlic, minced
1 teaspoon chili powder
1/2 teaspoon ground cumin
1/2 teaspoon paprika
Salt and pepper to taste
1/4 cup chopped fresh cilantro

For Assembling:

6 low-carb tortillas (or use lettuce wraps for an even lower-carb option)
1 cup shredded cheddar or Monterey Jack cheese
Chopped fresh cilantro and sliced avocado for garnish

Instructions:

Preheat your oven to 375°F (190°C).

To make the enchilada sauce, in a blender or food processor, combine the diced tomatoes, chopped onion, minced garlic, olive oil, chili powder, ground cumin, dried oregano, salt, and pepper. Blend until smooth.\
In a skillet, heat the olive oil over medium heat. Add the chopped onion and diced red bell pepper, and sauté until they become tender.
Stir in the minced garlic, chili powder, ground cumin, paprika, salt, and pepper. Cook for another minute until the spices are fragrant.
Add the shrimp to the skillet and cook for 2-3 minutes until they turn pink and are fully cooked. Be careful not to overcook the shrimp, as they can become tough.
Remove the skillet from the heat and stir in the chopped fresh cilantro.
To assemble the enchiladas, spoon some of the enchilada sauce onto the bottom of a baking dish.

Lay a low-carb tortilla flat and place a portion of the shrimp filling in the center. Roll up the tortilla and place it seam-side down in the baking dish. Repeat with the remaining tortillas and filling.
Pour the remaining enchilada sauce over the top of the assembled enchiladas.
Sprinkle shredded cheese over the enchiladas.
Bake the Low-Carb Shrimp Enchiladas in the preheated oven for 15-20 minutes, or until the cheese is melted and bubbly.
Garnish with chopped fresh cilantro and sliced avocado before serving

Crispy Keto Fish Tacos

Ingredients:

For the Crispy Fish:

1 lb white fish fillets (such as cod, tilapia, or halibut)
1/2 cup almond flour
1/4 cup grated Parmesan cheese
1 teaspoon paprika
1/2 teaspoon garlic powder
1/2 teaspoon onion powder
1/4 teaspoon cayenne pepper (adjust to your preferred level of spiciness)
Salt and pepper to taste
2 large eggs, beaten
Avocado oil or olive oil for frying

For the Taco Assembly:

Low-carb tortillas or lettuce wraps (for a lower-carb option)
Shredded lettuce
Sliced avocado
Sliced radishes
Chopped cilantro
Lime wedges
Keto-friendly salsa or hot sauce (optional)

Instructions:

Pat the fish fillets dry with paper towels and season with salt and pepper.
In a shallow dish, mix together the almond flour, grated Parmesan cheese, paprika, garlic powder, onion powder, cayenne pepper, salt, and pepper.
Dip each fish fillet into the beaten eggs, allowing any excess to drip off, and then coat it with the almond flour mixture, pressing it gently to adhere.
In a large skillet, heat enough avocado oil or olive oil over medium-high heat to shallow fry the fish.
Once the oil is hot, add the coated fish fillets to the skillet in batches (don't overcrowd the pan) and fry them for about 3-4 minutes on each side until they are golden and crispy. Remove the fried fish to a paper towel-lined plate to drain any excess oil.
Warm the low-carb tortillas or lettuce wraps in a separate dry skillet for a few seconds on each side, or as per the package instructions.
To assemble the Crispy Keto Fish Tacos, place a piece of crispy fish on each tortilla or lettuce wrap. Top the fish with shredded lettuce, sliced avocado, sliced radishes, and chopped cilantro.
Squeeze fresh lime juice over the toppings.
Optionally, drizzle some keto-friendly salsa or hot sauce over the tacos for added flavor and heat.
These Crispy Keto Fish Tacos are a delightful and satisfying meal that will make you feel like you're indulging in a restaurant-style treat while staying true to your low-carb or keto lifestyle. Enjoy these flavorful fish tacos with all the delicious toppings for a truly mouthwatering experience!

Seafood Paella

Ingredients:

1 lb shrimp, peeled and deveined
1 lb mussels, cleaned and debearded
1 lb squid, cleaned and sliced into rings
1/4 cup olive oil
1 onion, finely chopped
1 red bell pepper, diced
3 cloves garlic, minced
1 cup cauliflower rice
1/2 teaspoon saffron threads (optional)
1 teaspoon smoked paprika
1/2 teaspoon dried oregano
1/2 teaspoon ground cumin
1/4 teaspoon cayenne pepper (adjust to your preferred level of spiciness)
1 can (14 oz) diced tomatoes
1 3/4 cups chicken or seafood broth
1/4 cup dry white wine (optional)
Salt and pepper to taste
Lemon wedges and chopped fresh parsley for garnish

Instructions:

In a small bowl, crush the saffron threads (if using) and soak them in 2 tablespoons of warm water for about 10 minutes to release their flavor and color.
In a large paella pan or a wide skillet, heat the olive oil over medium heat.
Add the chopped onion and diced red bell pepper to the pan. Sauté until the onion becomes translucent and the pepper softens.
Stir in the minced garlic, smoked paprika, dried oregano, ground cumin, and cayenne pepper. Cook for another minute until the spices are fragrant.
Add the cauliflower rice to the pan and sauté for a few minutes until it starts to soften.
Pour in the diced tomatoes (with their juices) and the chicken or seafood broth. If using, add the soaked saffron threads with the water they were soaked in. Stir to combine.
Bring the mixture to a simmer and let it cook for about 10 minutes to allow the flavors to meld
Season with salt and pepper to taste.
Arrange the shrimp, mussels, and squid on top of the rice mixture in the pan.
Optionally, pour in the dry white wine over the seafood.
Cover the pan with a lid and let the Seafood Paella cook for about 10-15 minutes, or until the shrimp are pink, the mussels have opened, and the squid is tender.
Remove the pan from the heat and let it rest for a few minutes.
Garnish with lemon wedges and chopped fresh parsley before serving.
This low-carb Seafood Paella is a flavorful and satisfying dish that's perfect for seafood lovers following a low-carb or keto lifestyle. It's packed with a variety of delicious seafood and infused with aromatic spices, making it a delightful and impressive meal for any occasion. Enjoy it with family and friends for a truly special dining experience!

Thank you for choosing to embark on this culinary journey with me and for entrusting me with a small part of your kitchen adventures.

Your support and trust mean the world to me. Every recipe, every technique, and every story shared in this cookbook is a reflection of my passion for food and my desire to bring joy to your tables. Your decision to purchase this cookbook not only encourages me to continue sharing my culinary knowledge but also supports the countless hours of recipe testing, writing, and photography that went into its creation.

Wishing you many happy moments of deliciousness and culinary creativity!

For Zian And Milan, who brings smiles to my face and joy to my heart every day

www.ingramcontent.com/pod-product-compliance
Lightning Source LLC
Chambersburg PA
CBHW081236080526
44587CB00022B/3955